Triumph Motorcycle Restoration

Timothy Remus
&
Garry Chitwood

Published by:
Wolfgang Publications Inc.
Stillwater, MN 55082
www.wolfpub.com

Legals

First published in 2007 by Wolfgang Publications Inc.,
PO Box 223, Stillwater MN 55082

© Timothy Remus, 2007/2014

ISBN: 1-929133-42-1
ISBN-13: 978-1-929133-42-0

Printed and bound in U.S.A.

Triumph Motorcycle Restoration

Acknowledgements

What you hold in your hands is a book written not by Timothy Remus, or even Timothy Remus and Garry Chitwood. It's a book written by a team. And thanks go out to each member of that team.

Garry Chitwood is a quiet man, but if you shut up long enough he will tell you anything you want to know about Triumphs. Because there isn't much about Triumphs that Garry doesn't know. Lots of people know the numbers, how big the engines are or how much the bike weighs or when they stopped using the girder fork. Garry knows most of that, but he also knows things that only a good mechanic knows. Like the best way to slide the cylinder down onto the pistons, or how to shorten a brake cable for those occasions when you don't have exactly the correct cable.

Ryan Bissett didn't grow up with Triumphs, he's far too young for that. Ryan discovered Triumphs when he started working for Bobby Sullivan. Though the youngest member of the team, Ryan is old enough to listen and learn, and he doesn't mind getting his hands dirty. In fact, Ryan is so smitten with the old twins he sold the crotch-rocket Honda and relies on an old Bonneville for his two-wheeled transportation.

The man who keeps Garry and Ryan excited about, and working on, Triumphs is Bobby Sullivan. Bobby contracted the disease years ago when he wrenched and raced Triumphs. You would think by now that Bobby would be burned out on Triumphs, that the passion might have dimmed, but instead he seems to get more excited as the years go by.

A few other Triumph nuts contributed as well, including Randy Baxter from Baxter Cycle and Mitch Klempf from Klempf's British Parts. Finally I have to thank Jacki Mitchell and Deb Shade for putting the book together and insuring the photos look as good as they do, and my wife Mary Lanz for proof reading and moral support.

Timothy Remus

Introduction

This is certainly not the first Triumph restoration book to be published. It's not even the second. I do believe however, that it's the most photo-intensive restoration book ever published.

My idea was simple, photograph two unit-650 Triumph twins as they are converted from a pile of parts into running motorcycles. Sort the images into logical progressions, do a layout, and give the layouts back to the guys who did the assemblies – and let them write the captions.

Service manuals are great and the good ones convey a wealth of information. You might even want one to accompany this how-to book. What a typical service manual is missing though, is enough photos and illustrations to truly illuminate the subject, especially for non-professional mechanics.

So while this book might be missing some torque specifications or the point-gap for the '63 Bonneville, it has real photos of real people assembling two bikes and one engine/transmission.

In place of a written description of the changes that occurred from 1959 to 1970, we've included a gallery of Triumphs. In the center of the book you will find 24 pages that show left and right side views of the most significant models offered during those years. A significant number of old Triumphs spend their days sitting in the garage or the office. And while they are certainly as beautiful as any bronze sculpture by Remington, they no longer leak oil on the ground in front of the local bar or drive in and the unique sound of a Triumph twin seldom bounces off the canyon walls of downtown Minneapolis, Detroit, or Los Angeles. No longer do Triumphs race Nortons or Harleys when the light on Broadway turns green. In an effort to reverse this trend, we offer up a chapter dedicated to keeping the Triumphs running. It's not hard or even expensive. Mostly it takes a good charging circuit and the right attitude.

This book is dedicated to buying, repairing, and (I hope) riding old Triumphs.

Chapter One

Disassembly of the '69

First You Have to Take it Apart

According to Garry Chitwood the first thing to do before you disassemble a bike is to get it up in the air on a table or lift. Next, you need a couple of boxes, each one with its own number. Number one could be engine parts, two would be the oil tank and side covers, number three for the

fender, brackets and wheels... you get the idea. Garry goes on to recommend separate boxes for anything that needs to be cad plated.

The whole idea is to keep everything organized with an eye toward the various additional steps many of the parts will have to go through.

This '69 was found at an estate sale in Missouri. It was covered by a pack rat's old pile of magazines. The pile was so big they didn't even know it was underneath. This probably saved it from further destruction. When it got to Massachusetts we couldn't believe it was in such good condition. Some said just clean it up and ride it. But we knew we had to go all out. Here we go.

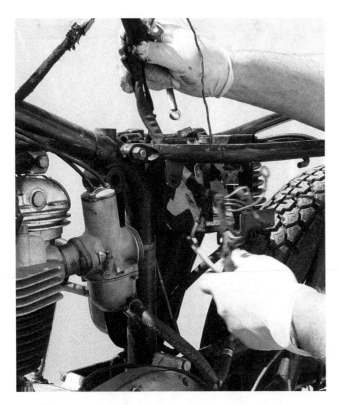

Bobby removes the old dirty harness, some wires are melted, have been cut or repaired. Also the cloth cover is ripped and torn in a lot of places.

Once the wheels are off the bike, for example, pull them apart and then put the rims in the chrome box and identify any bad spokes or bearings.

Next, Garry likes to take the motor apart and add any nuts that need to be cad plated to the "cad" box. In terms of being able to put Humpty Dumpty back together again, a whole slew of decent digital pictures are sure to help later. With the external nuts and bolts in a cad box Garry takes the engine the rest of the way apart, and sets the components carefully in another group of boxes. You need to inspect all those engine parts as another step in the overhaul procedure, or have someone else inspect the pistons, cylinders and all the rest to determine exactly what you will need to make the old 650 run like new.

Garry and Bobby Sullivan use a cad plater who handles only commercial accounts. If you're new to all this and don't have a relationship with a cad plater, ask the local chrome shop, many do cad plating as well, or know someone who does. There is no need to pre-treat the parts to be plat-

This is one scuzzy old Triumph, anyone who thinks you can make a nice restored bike out of something like this must be a true optimist, or they're smokin".

Overall this is in great shape. After we take the tank off we can get a good look at the engine. Not bad at all.

Next we remove the seat to get some light into the rear frame. She's really dirty, and the harness has some problems. The good thing is all the hardware looks untouched. Rare!

As we clear things out of the way, we found the old twin-tone horn relay and horn bracket. We will have to find the horns to do it right. It won't be easy.

Bobby removes the rear frame. The ass end is done. This bike is coming apart very well. No problems.

The rear tire and fender were removed. The rear rim was very nice and would be rechromed. The rear fender and chain guard were both cracked and will need some work.

With the front wheel out of the way, this special tool is used to loosen the dust covers. Sometimes a little heat helps. Also he uses a long ratchet extension to keep the lower legs from spinning.

With the oil tank out of the way, Bobby removes the swing fork. This was one of the greasiest rear sections we've seen. But that's a good thing for preservation.

Unscrew the member from the dust excluder and pull down. It should slide right off. Watch out for oil spray when pulling it all the way off.

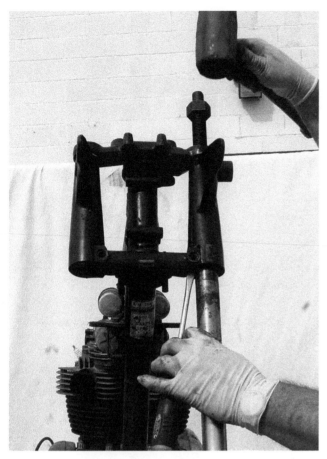

This special tool for the stanchion makes the removal a snap. It's okay to tap a screwdriver into the slot on the bottom lug. Just don't over do it to avoid damage to the metal.

ed, as most platers use a strip tank as one of the first steps.

There are alternative coatings, including zinc and Bright-dip. Brite-dip, often used on late model Harleys, is what Garry calls a cousin in the cad-plating family. Both Brite-dip and zinc are considerably brighter than cad, so if you want a 100 point restoration, only cad plating will do.

For the painted items, Garry puts the parts in two piles, explaining as he does, "I put the chassis parts and engine mounting brackets in a series of boxes that will go to the powder coater. Then things like the horns for the headlight and the side covers go into a separate box to be sent to the painter. The powder coat is much better than it was a few years ago, but it still isn't good enough for parts that need that nice smooth surface."

The telescopic fork parts fall right off. Bobby used a little heat to help. This is an important step to make disassembly easy.

Here he removes the rockers. Taking his time because the hardware on this motor appears untouched and we're going to reuse it. Nothing better than the original hardware in great condition.

The head is also in perfect shape. Pull it off slowly. We find STD pistons in the jug. Can't wait to put this '69 back together, though it will take months to source the parts and bring her back to original.

Chapter Two

Assemble & Restore the '69

The 1969 Bonnie goes back Together

Putting together a Triumph motorcycle may not be rocket science but it does require follow through and good attention to detail. As good as we think this book is, you probably want a service manual as well. Garry Chitwood likes to start with the bike on a hoist or table of some kind. The stands shown here are ideal as they leave the bike fully accessible.

Garry and Bobby have taken to powder coating the frame, primarily because the powder paint is so much more durable. The rest of the black parts were painted with conventional liquid paint at the nearby Shadley Brothers/AutoTec shop.

A great looking old Triumph, especially if you take a look at the "before" picture on page six.

Be sure to chase the threads on all bolt holes and clean them out with some air. This is something we do to all stud holes before reassembly. This little step will help save many headaches down the road.

Speaking of paint, a good paint job gets on all the surfaces, even the threaded holes in the frame. Which is why all those holes have to be cleaned out with the correct tap. Again, make sure you are using the right tap, some threads on a '69 are SAE and some are C.E.I. (see Chapter Three for more on fasteners).

Unless you have a really good memory, it's a good idea to take lots of digital photos before and during the disassembly, so you can get everything put back together again. When Garry and Bobby disassemble a bike, they take it apart to the last nut and bolt. Even the wheels are completely disassembled so the rims can be sent out for a fresh coat of chrome and the spokes can be cad plated. For tires they use the original Dunlop K70s, though the new ones come from Japan, not England. And don't go riding on those old weather checked originals, even if they do have lots of tread left.

(continued on page 16)

Here are most of the parts needed for the restoration. We have a lot of work to do to get this Bonnie back together.

Installing the center stand, we begin by filing the holes where the pivot bolt goes in. Tapping the center stand helps it go together easily.

Close up shows the pivot bolt/tab washer/nut. Take a small punch and fold the tabs over the nut after it is tightened. If done correctly each tab will be folded over on a different flat.

Installing studs in the front frame. Double nut the stud and tighten. Tapping the holes in the frame earlier made this go smoothly.

Here we line up of the rear frame, ready to push the 3/8 inch British stud through. Spring washers and nuts are used on either end of the stud.

Prop stand pivot bolt and self-locking nut. File the inside of the lug and the prop stand to help the pivot bolt slide through easily.

When tightening bolts always use the box end of the wrench to prevent rounding off the corners.

Installation of the rear frame to the front frame including the bolt/spring-washer. As you can see it's best to have your center stand on before you install the rear frame or it will be a tight fit.

Here we're installing the bonded bush in the top lug. We're using a special must-have tool for the installation. Be sure to clean out any over-spray before you start installing the bonded bush.

Here we prep for the swing fork bolt. During this part of reassembly the file and tap set will make the job go so much easier.

Installing the sleeve, we used new pivot bushings in the swing fork. Sometimes the sleeve needs a little tap to go in.

We use grease on the sleeve to help it go into the swing fork bushings. Be sure to check the sleeves for wear before the reassembly.

Flanged washer with o-ring, the end cap on the swing fork. These retain the grease in the swing fork.

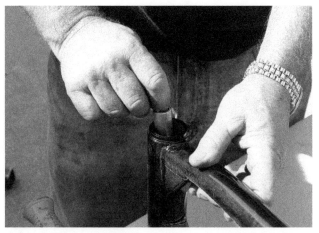

The distance tube fits into the sleeves. Drop it into the swing fork, and make sure it seats into the sleeve on the other side properly.

When installing the swing fork the extra hands sure do help. You may have to file some paint away so the flanged washers fit between the fork and frame.

With the center stand and rear frame done, we install the damper units to the swinging fork and rear frame, with the original hardware.

We snug the sleeve nut and then use a torque wrench set at 15 ft. lbs. for the final adjustment.

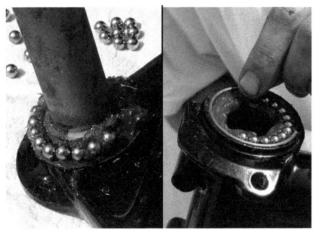

We set 20, 1/4 inch steel balls into the top and 20 into the bottom steering race cup using plenty of grease to retain the balls.

Inserting the pinch bolt into the top lug. The nut for the pinch bolt should have a dome on it.

After the balls are installed, Bobby inserts the middle lug, pushes down the dust cover, puts the top lug on top of the dust cover and hand tightens the fork stem sleeve nut.

Bobby sets the stanchion covers in place and puts the chrome pinch bolts into the middle lug. We are smiling because Bobby said, "maybe we should have left her the way we found her."

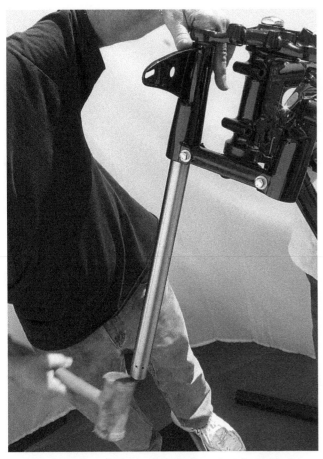

1. With the top lug pinch bolt finger tight and the middle lug pinch bolts loose, Bobby taps the stanchion in place. Sometimes they go in easily, sometimes they don't.

4. Bobby is holding the lower leg upside down, the restrictor is up inside the 5/8 socket which is on the end of a long extension. The flange bolt and washer are in Bobby's right hand.

2. We put Honda bond on the restrictor to help prevent the good old Triumph oil leak. The restrictor will end up inside the fork's lower leg.

3. The restrictor is mounted in a 5/8 inch socket before being positioned up inside the lower leg.

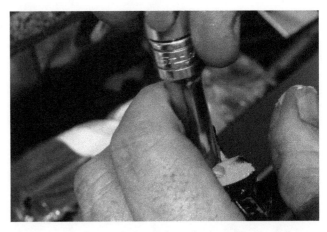

5. Now the flange bolt with sealing washer can be screwed to the restrictor. As a final precaution against leaks, the recess for the flange bolt will be filled with black silicone.

Here we have the parts that go in the dust excluder, 2 plain washers, the bigger one goes on top to protect the seal from the spring, one fork seal and one O-ring. The spring part of the seal faces down.

The fork seal installation tool will help you install the seal straight and without damage, which is what can happen when you use a socket instead of this tool.

Here we have a the shuttle valve, bearing nut and circlip. We were able to reuse the original shuttle valve.

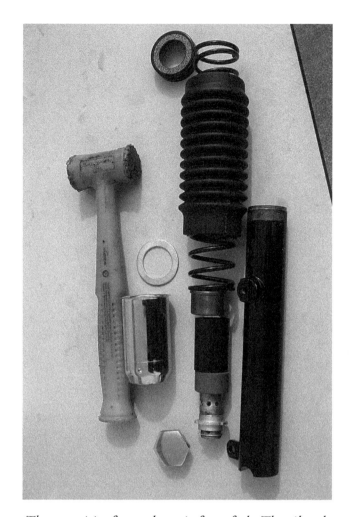

The necessities for a telescopic front fork. The oil seal, plain washer and O-ring are already installed in the dust excluder sleeve nut.

If you're lucky enough to have a wiring harness in good condition, go ahead and use it again. "Finding a good original harness is tough," says Garry Chitwood, "some of the books have wiring schematics so you can repair the harness if it's not damaged too badly. John Healy has some aftermarket harnesses that are pretty good, and if you really look you might be able to find a nice NOS harness.

When it comes to the fork assembly, it's a good idea to replace the seals, the gaitors, the tubes and bushings. "The external-type springs should probably be replaced too," advises Garry. "The service manuals give a dimension for an uncompressed spring, so you can tell if they've lost their tension. I like to use 20 or 30 weight fork oil, the amounts are listed in the service manuals."

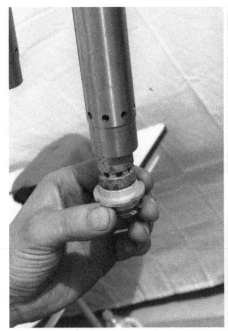

This is where the shuttle valve ends up. It's the last step on the front end assembly. He checks here to make sure the bearing nut threads into the stanchion with no problems.

The first step is the cork washer, then the spring abutment and the spring.

We like to put the telescopic gaiter on with the spring. It makes it easier than trying to slide it up when done.

With the fork oil seal installed, drop the oil seal washer (the bigger of the two) into the dust excluder sleeve nut.

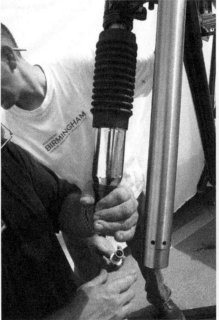

Slide the dust excluder up. With the O-ring and washer already in place, push the top bearing into the dust excluder.

Follow up with the damping sleeve, lower bearing and shuttle valve assembly. It's nice to have three hands to keep the springs up while tightening the bearing nut.

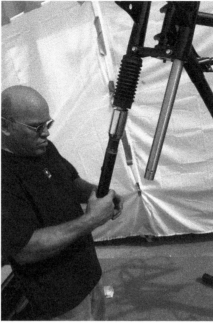

The telescopic internals are in place and ready for the lower leg or bottom member.

Bobby slides the lower member over the bearings with the help of some oil.

Don't forget that cork washer or it will sound like your front end is going to fall off when you hit the first bump in the road.

This wrench is a must to do the job right. So many dust excluders are junk because of chisels, water pump pliers or whatever somebody could find to take them off.

Use some light oil to help slide the gaiter over the dust excluder and the top abutment.

The telescopic front fork is almost done. Don't forget to torque the stanchion pinch bolts to 25 ft. lbs.

Here is the handlebar eyelet with the upper hemispherical washer, the steady rubber (which uses a small inside spacer) and the metal cup.

That screwdriver is dangerous. The cost of the handlebars and rechroming isn't worth the risk. Luckily Bobby has a steady hand!

The handlebar eyebolts, mounted on top of a cup to hold the steady-rubber with a spacer in the middle and a hemispherical washer on top.

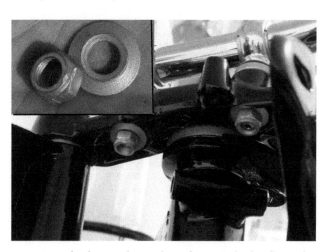

Drop in the hemispherical washers with the flat side facing up and snug up the self locking nuts.

The packing piece isn't always that easy to push into the eyebolt with your fingers. Find something to tap it into place that won't scratch the chrome.

Fill the stanchion with 190cc each of fork oil and then tighten up the cap nuts. The Honda bond and black silicone used during assembly should keep the oil where it belongs.

With the metalistic bushings in the speedometer-tachometer mounting bracket, it's time to install the instruments rebuilt by Nisonger.

The brake shoes are in place. Next we install the black, lever return spring, the front brake cam levers, rear lever, washers and nuts.

Here we have NOS brake shoes, the anchor plate, return springs and brake cam are all ready to go. Be sure to replace the shoes if the bike will be a rider.

Bobby installs the anchor plate gauze for the air scoop, secured by taptite screws and plain washers.

Put your abutment pad on each brake shoe. Grease up the brake plate where the shoes pivot. Grease the brake cam, some grease on the return spring doesn't hurt either.

This is where the NOS brake shoes come in handy. The anchor plate slides right into the brake drum. Sometimes the new shoes need some sanding.

Only snug the brake anchor plate nut. Too tight and the wheel won't spin freely.

Here we have the catch plunger, spring and washer in place. Just bend the split pin and we're done.

The front wheel is on, torque the spindle cap bolts to 25 ft. lbs. Having the proper bolt with correct lettering on the head is a must on any proper restoration.

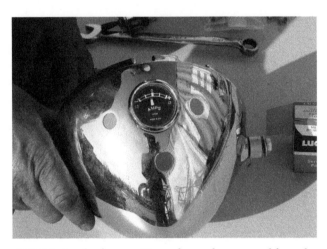

NOS is in the house. How about that new old stock ammeter. The box is on the right. It's all about the little touches.

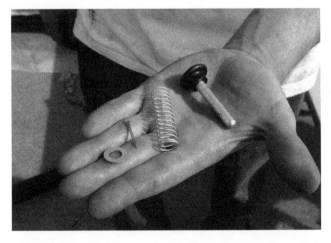

The seat catch plunger, spring, very thin washer, and split pin are ready to go.

If you have the ammeter a NOS lighting switch has to go with it. This bucket is almost there. Don't forget the aluminum washer under the nut.

Here we have the headlight spacer used between stanchion covers and headlamp shell. Note the plain washer and bolt, which will be torqued to 10 ft. lbs.

We had new old stock fender stays rechromed. The original fender bolts, plain washers and self locking nuts are used to put it all together.

We had NOS warning lights, ammeter lighting switch, but the rubber seals were rotten and cracked, so we called Coventry Spares.

With the bike's original front end, the NOS front fender and fender brackets it all goes together and lines up with no headaches, no files, and no scratches.

These are both aftermarket, the one on the right is a bad copy, the dead giveaway is the "Made In England" script, the real one is on page 21.

This control body was removed from the original '69 as was the front brake lever. The fulcrum screw, lever clamp screws and control body bolt were replaced by NOS.

The control body comes together with a NOS spring washer, rechromed body, cap and NOS replated bolt.

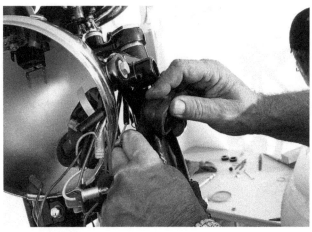

We replaced the ignition switch cover with an after-market unit. The NOS covers are so old they sometimes split or crack after a short period of time.

This is a NOS heat sink and plug. The original '69 had broken fins and was black. Bobby's parts collection NOS heat sinks are not painted. Were there factory black painted heat sinks?

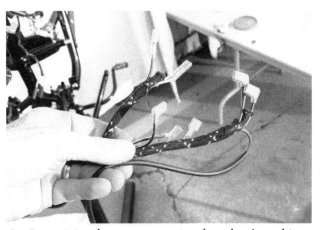

Re-Pop wiring harnesses are nice, but there's nothing better than NOS. The noticeable difference between the two are the Lucas connectors and the insulating covers.

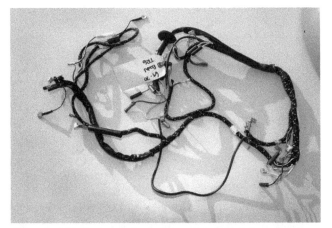

We were lucky enough to have this NOS harness in stock. This has to be the holy grail of a perfect restoration. A must-have to do it right and a hard item to find.

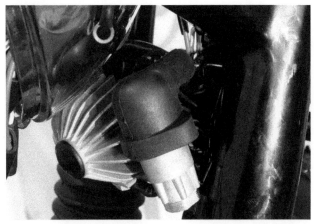

The ignition switch is in place and ready to drop in. It's a little tight to get in place with the headlight bucket installed, but possible.

It is time for the ignition lock to go into the switch. Notice the gap between the stanchion cover and the top lug. This is normal.

First we put the oil tank bracket and a grommet on. It helps to hold up the tank while getting it into position. Then we hand tighten the bolt and spring washer to the frame.

Here we ground the wiring harness to the tachometer. Scrape away some of the paint on the mounting bracket to insure a good ground.

Also, install the spigot rubber into the oil tank before pushing in the screwed pegs. Some grease helps it slide into place. You don't want that screwdriver to slip off and scratch the oil tank. Take it slow.

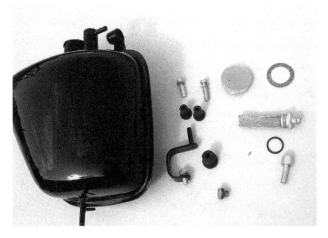

The oil tank is ready to go in with new rubber and re-cad plated hardware, rechromed filler cap and new joint washers.

The rubber washers go in between the front and rear straps that support the battery carrier. Do not over tighten or the rubber will pancake.

The original battery carrier was still good. Too many times they are pitted from the lack of a battery vent tube, which allows the acid to drain onto the bottom of the carrier.

A NOS Lucas rectifier has to be used to do it right. Big bucks maybe, but it's worth it in the long run. No shortcuts.

Pull apart the battery carrier and pull it down into place. Sometimes you may have to regap the fold-overs on top to help compensate for the new paint.

Hand tighten the rectifier so that you can rotate it while connecting the wiring harness. We have yet to see one with consistent length.

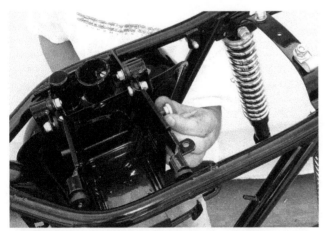

The battery carrier is in. This sleeve nut is a nice touch. Too many times it is replaced by a nut during a restoration. Wrong!

The oil tank filter is put in place. We used a NOS fiber washer. Some are black, green, red, gray or tan. They are all NOS. Sometimes the filter is so thinned from age that the screen falls apart during plating .

How To Buy an Old Triumph

Tucked away in the small town of Marne, Iowa, halfway between Des Moines and Omaha, is Baxter Cycle. If you walk through the front doors into the new showroom, you'll likely find Randy Baxter behind the counter talking to a customer. And while the bikes on the show floor are gleaming new Triumphs, the really good stuff is down the hall in the back room.

There you will find over a hundred vintage English motorcycles, everything from Triumph Bonnevilles to the occasional Vincent Black Shadow. Among the variety of bikes, one marque dominates, and that is Triumph. Given Randy's long history of buying and selling, he seemed the perfect person to provide a little help for anyone looking to buy a new/old Triumph.

Randy, give us a little background. How long have you been in business as Baxter Cycle and how many bikes do you think you've sold in that time?

I've been selling and servicing all the British bikes since the mid seventies. In that time I've sold at least four to five thousand bikes.

If I'm a first time Triumph buyer, would it be better to buy one of the later bikes?

For a first-time person, the '64 to '79 bikes would be a good way to go. Parts and manuals are readily available, they're easier to maintain and repair.

The value of the '71 and later bikes seems to be coming up. We found a nice original '71, 5 speed

Walking into the back room at Baxter Cycle is like turning a kid loose in the candy store, the store with the really good candy. The kind your mother said you couldn't have. The stock turns over constantly, so what you find one week will be different by the next.

How To Buy an Old Triumph

recently and put it on our web site as a feature bike – and we had people fighting over it. If you're over 6 feet tall, those '71 and later bikes will fit you really well. Mechanically they are good, the culmination of a lot of R&D done up to that time. The down side is they are not as attractive, and might be too tall for shorter riders.

I would not buy a pre-unit Triumph as a first bike. They are much more complicated, just the gas tank includes a huge number of parts, and those parts are harder to find and more expensive. You are also dealing with magnetos and generators, The bikes are fine, but not as a first Triumph.

If I'm going to buy an old Triumph, how do I know it's in good mechanical condition?

I tell people to ride the bike first. Take your helmet and jacket when you go to look at a bike and ride it 10 or 20 miles. That will tell you what you want to know. I have a customer who's an old Harley-Davidson dealer. When he comes up he will ride a dozen bikes, and he buys the ones that run the best and that's a smart way to do it.

If I'm buying more of a collector bike, how do I know if it is assembled from the right parts?

The older the Triumph, (this Speed Twin dates from 1939) the more difficult and expensive it is to restore and/or keep running on a daily basis.

The later oil-in-frame bikes like this 1978-1/2 T140E were never as popular as the earlier bikes, but they come with a 750cc engine, five-speed transmission and a disc brake.

How To Buy an Old Triumph

After thirty years in the business of selling used British bikes, Randy Baxter recommends a thorough inspection and a 20 mile ride, before you buy.

It would be good to have an expert's opinion on that. You can also go by who you are buying it from. If it's a reputable dealer that's OK, with eBay, once you buy the bike it's all over. We see a lot of bad eBay deals on restored bikes.

It's important to look at things like the fasteners. Are they uniform or are they hardware-store bolts. Look at the wiring harness too, is it a taped up piece of junk or is it a nice cloth-bound harness. Look under the seat, under the gas tank. What kind of chain did they use. If it's a Reynolds or a Diamond chain it's likely they used good stuff on the rest of the bike too.

Where do people get screwed, what do they do wrong?

They make the mistake of becoming infatuated with the photo on the computer screen. People get suckered in by that photo. As a seller, you can do a lot with a good camera and some nice lighting.

We recently had a guy bring us a '68 Bonneville, supposedly this was the nicest restored Bonneville in the world. It came out of Canada, he bought it and had it shipped to his home. Once he got it there it wouldn't start so he called us. Before he even had it unloaded I could see that the engine number was altered, and the frame number too. I told him, "every

The frame and engine numbers must match, and show no evidence of being altered. If in doubt, get a Triumph expert to inspect the bike and the numbers.

How To Buy an Old Triumph

nickel you spend with us is money down the drain, just ship it back to the guy you bought it from."

So you have to watch the numbers, verify that the engine and frame numbers are correct, some of these guys are getting really good at doctoring numbers. You can fix anything else about the bike, but if it has altered numbers you can't fix that. Make sure that the engine and frame numbers are correct and matching. When you buy the bike, have a written agreement with the seller that if the numbers are not matching you can rescind the deal.

There are also matching case numbers that you can only see by sliding under the bike or laying it on its side. The left and right cases should have the same number. That will tell you if it was ever blown up so bad they had to replace a case half.

Do you want to talk about auctions and the best way to buy a bike at an auction?

The best advice is pretty simple. Get there early enough to really look at the bikes carefully and check the numbers, the fasteners and the overall condition. Make notes of the bikes you're interested in, allow yourself enough time before the auction, write down the top price you would pay, and don't forget to keep track of the buyer's premium.

You need to discipline yourself. Sometimes you see a bike roll across the stage and it's a bike that looks good and you don't have any notes. So you get all excited about the bike and end up paying too much. When situations like that come up you need to just sit on your hands.

Ask the auction people what

Randy Baxter started out selling and repairing old Triumphs when the smart money was on the Japanese brands.

they know about the bike and ask if the owner is present. You can learn a lot from the owner. Even if the owner isn't there, you should check to see if it's a reputable shop or an individual selling the bike. Be careful if the bike is recently imported from another country, some of those have a lot of miles on the clock, and there may be issues with the title.

Any final words of wisdom?

Titles. The title is always the fly in the ointment. Make sure the title is transferable. Some are really old, make sure the title you get can be transferred, and converted to a current title in your state.

How to Buy photos: Joseph Murphy

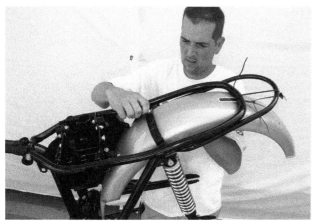

Connect the rear fender to the bridge, and then the bolt and nut to the bracket in front of the swing fork. I like to use zip ties to hold up the lifting handle while setting the fender in place.

She's starting to look like a Triumph, not just a pile of parts on a table that took months to recondition, repaint and get ready for reassembly. Nice!

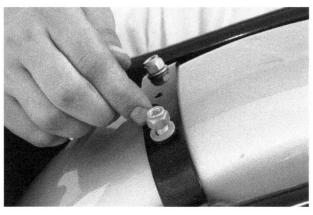

Use plain washers with self locking nuts. Only hand tighten the nuts until the fender is completely lined up. Don't forget the clip for the extension pipe where my finger is.

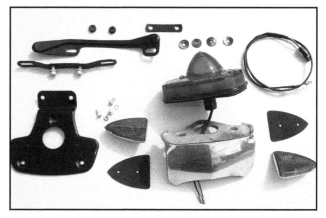

Here we have all the parts to put the tail lamp back together, NOS lens, lens gasket, rubber mats, red reflectors and tail lamp lead.

We used the original rear fender and lifting handle and it still does not line up. That is why you must leave your fender hardware loose and nuts finger tight until everything is in place.

For installing the tail lamp plate to the adapter we used the original plate and repolished adapter. They go together no problem. File the paint around the screw holes so that you get a good ground.

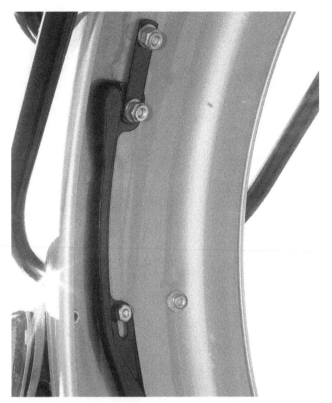

The tail lamp wiring protector and backing plate are in place under the rear fender. Not shown here is the clip for the extension pipe that connects to the lifting handle bolt and nut.

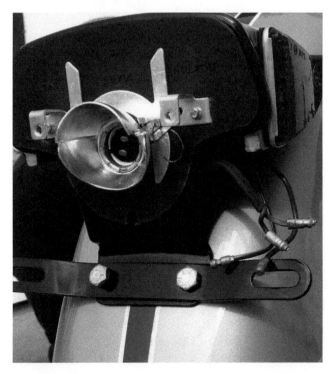

The assembled rear taillight mounted on the rear is ready for wiring.

The flip side of the tail lamp adapter with stud in place. Use a star washer before putting on the nut.

The tail lamp assembly is ready to mount to the rear fender using only the original adapter and plate and re-cad hardware. All rubber, reflectors and lens are NOS.

Routing the tail lamp lead through the rubber grommet on the rear fender, bring it up to the plug on the harness behind the battery carrier.

The original chainguard was replaced with a re-pop due to damage. Install the screw and self locking nuts before setting the chainguard in place. The parts catalog shows the bolts on the outside. Not correct.

We decided to use a NOS Smith's speedo gearbox. It looks a little rough, but it's fresh out of the box. This is how it was. A real nice touch to this restoration.

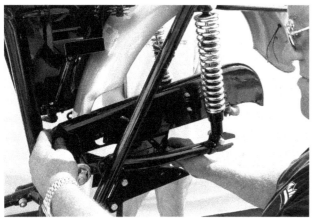

Bobby sets the chainguard in place with ease. No rear rim makes it easy. Do not tighten yet. You will have to lift the rear up to put the rim and tire on.

The inner nut is snugged to the anchor plate. We reused the chain adjusters and end plate, but the spindle nuts we replaced with NOS because some "mechanic" used a pipe wrench on the originals.

Brake shoes are on. Use some grease on the brake cam and return springs. Also the thrust pads. The rest of the parts are lined up and ready to go.

Leaving the stepped bolt loose, Garry holds up the chainguard for Bobby. This helps clear the sprocket while pushing the wheel spindle in place.

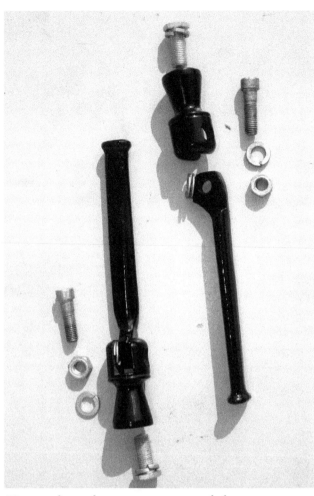

The refurbished Lucas stop lamp switch. We take them apart, re-cad the arm, repaint the top, and clean up the bottom and insides. We top it off with two self locking nuts with the dashes on the sides.

Here we have the passenger pegs and the correct mounting hardware.

The original seat pan was almost cracked in half from lifting the bike using the seat rail instead of the lifting handle. Bobby had a used original seat pan in good shape which Garry painted.

This is the area where the pan is either cracked or almost falling off due to lifting the bike by the seat rail. A one year design. We had the original seat rail rechromed.

We had our seat recovered by Coventry Spares using an original pan. Re-pops are a dead giveaway. The check wire is in place, sometimes they need to be shortened.

With the motor in, Bobby steps back to think about what's next. We are about three days into two bikes. A whole lot of work, and fun when you see a pile of parts turn into a finished motorcycle.

The twinseat falls right in line with the seat catch plunger because the seat pan is original and the front and rear hinges to the seat pan were not bent like they usually are.

She is looking like a brand new '69. At this point we are maybe halfway through, but there's a ton of pieces left and a lot of work ahead.

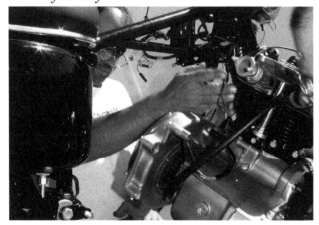

We like to bring the motor in on the right side of the bike, lifting the rear of the motor up to clear the oil tank, getting the rear past everything, then setting the front in place.

We had the original exhaust pipes rechromed. Here Bobby checks to make sure that the exhaust slides over the pipe adapter with no hang ups, before sliding the exhaust pipe clip into place.

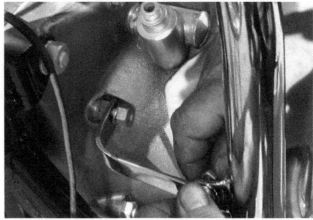

The exhaust pipe tie falls right into place. We had the ties rechromed with the pipes. Re-pop parts never align this easily.

Nice shot of the silencer stay. Some restorations are missing the stay. One of the little things it takes to do it right. Also, that hardware looks perfect.

Note the coupling pipe, caps, and clips. Auto advance and contact breaker plate are in place. The NOS cylinder head is on and ready for some rocker boxes.

This is an easy way to push the rocker spindle into place. Using a socket on the oil feed side, close the vice nice and slow, don't force the parts together.

Bobby sets the inlet rocker into place. It's important to line up the push rods into the rocker ball pins. We like to put some grease on the tappets to hold the push rods in place.

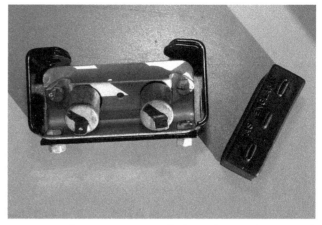

NOS condensers were installed on the condenser pack bracket mounted to the horn bracket, using the re-cad hardware that will be protected by a NOS cover.

We adjust the tappets to .002 inch for the intake and .004 for the exhaust.

Condensers and horn bracket center between the tank mount. Bracket is held in place using bolts, shake-proof washers and nuts. Rocker inspection caps and joint washers are also installed.

Exhaust/inlet rockers go on before installing engine torque stays. The cylinder bolts are torqued down. Headbolts, 3/8 inch BS, are tightened to 35 ft. lbs., 5/16 inch BS center are tightened to 15 ft. lbs.

Bobby hooks up the rubber connector to the rocker oil feed pipe. It is bent down behind the oil tank.

Here you can see the routing of the oil lines.

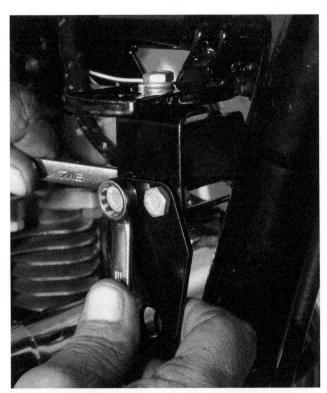

Installing the mounting bracket for the horn, note the use of the box end of the wrench.

The rocker oil feed is connected to the oil tank as shown. The flexible connector is in place. Note the correct clip. No hose clamps here. Next the tank filter and feed pipe will be installed.

Here we're installing the speed nut for the left side cover.

We used a NOS horn relay and relay stay for those hard to find twin tone horns - that were missing from the '69 when we got it.

These horns are next to impossible to find and expensive if you do. Bobby tells a story about taking them off and throwing them away when he was a Triumph mechanic. Lucky for us Chitwood had a pair!

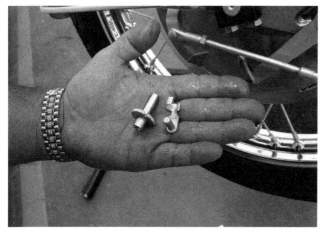

Bobby holds the cable adjuster and nut. He also has the correct pivot pin to connect the front brake cable.

Garry is checking the amount of free play in the front brake, this is a little too much.

The front brake cable fork end falls right into place. Perfect length. Not too long or too short. Next he will install the pivot pin into the brake cam lever.

AMAL CARBS

Though they were much maligned back in the day, Garry runs the Amal carbs and has very little trouble. "The only thing you run into is a worn bore and a loose slide. You can either have a sleeve installed or just buy a new carburetor. When they are loose like that it's hard to get them to idle down, especially when there are two of them." (See Chapter Three for more on Amals.)

If you're going to ride the restoration when it's done Garry recommends better rear shocks, even if they don't look exactly like the originals, a sealed beam headlight and a new, higher output charging circuit.

The important thing is to get the bike back together. "I think that with all the photos we've put in this book, a person at home with some mechanical aptitude can probably do 70 or 80 percent of the work, without having to send it out to an expert for the whole thing."

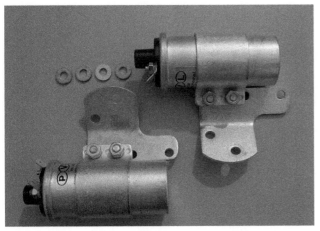

Coils and brackets are ready to go on. We used 12-volt coils, made in Germany, and purchased from Coventry Spares.

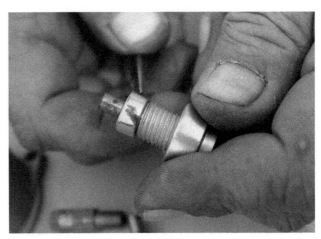

Garry tightening the needle jet to the jet holder.

The top end is done. Horns are on and wired, coils connected to the harness, and notice the correct insulating blocks on the carburetor adapters.

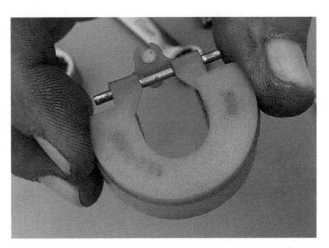

We reused the original float and needle. They were still good. Gotta try to save money somewhere.

Here we have the basics ready to rebuild the carburetor. I like to clean the body parts by putting it in a cold parts immersion bucket, but not for too long.

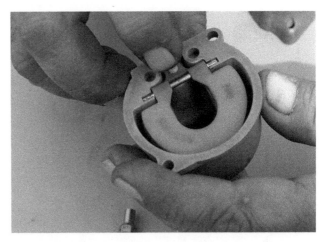

Garry sets the float into the chamber making sure the needle doesn't fall out and float spindle moves freely.

The main jet is installed into the jet holder and the float chamber is ready to be attached to the mixing chamber.

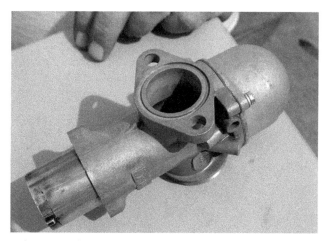

Always make sure the throttle valve slides in and out of the mixing chamber smoothly. Sometimes they're warped.

We replaced the throttle stop screw because of wear in the screwdriver slot.

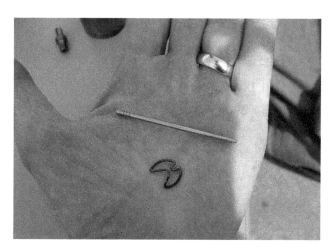

Here we have a new Amal needle and needle clip.

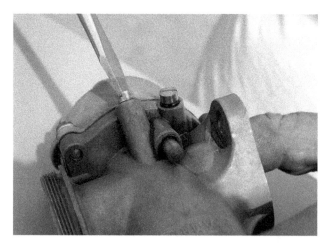

Ease the stop screw and air adjusting screw into the mixing chamber. New Amal carburetors have a much larger tickler on them.

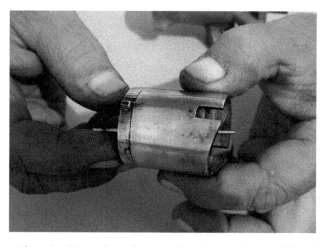

After checking the valve, set the clip in the middle of the needle and slide it in.

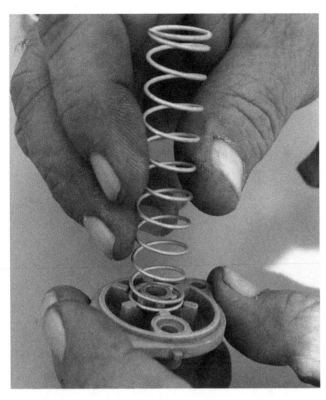

We like to check the fit of the return spring to the chamber top. There are so many springs around our shop that are different, it's a good idea to check.

This is the main jet installed in the holder.

Here you can see the filter assembly before it's bolted to the bottom of the float bowl.

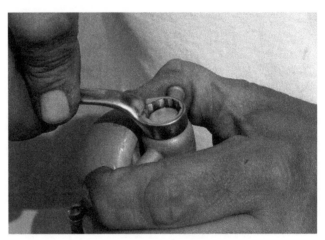

Garry snugs the filter onto the float chamber. The banjo bolt was replaced. The old one was abused by a 1/2 inch wrench, they are actually 5/16 inch.

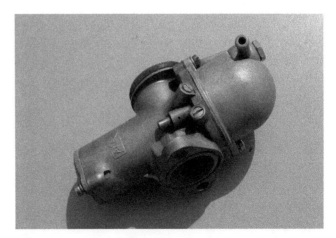

Here we have the assembled 930 carburetor.

This is what we mean by zinc coating being too bright. The spigot on the left is zinc plated, the one on the right is cad plated.

These are re-pop adapters, using the correct cups, and insulating ring, later replaced with originals.

This is the correct hardware to mount the carburetor. Don't over tighten the nuts.

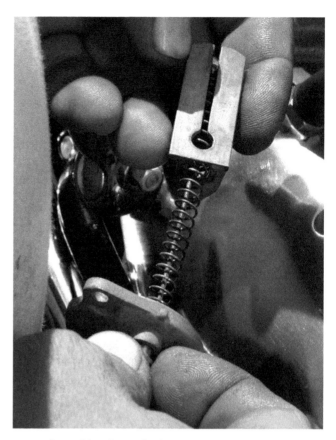

Run the cables through the mixing chamber top into the spring and push them together. Lock the cable into the air slide.

We've installed the left side carb, which is a nice fit even with the new carb spigot.

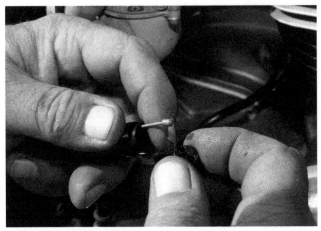

The air cable assembly is hooked up here. Make sure the junction box is free of cracks and slides back and forward when closed.

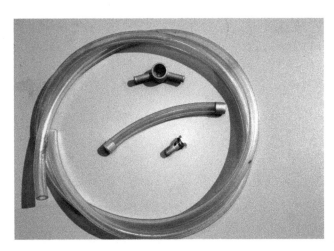

Bulk fuel line and assorted parts.

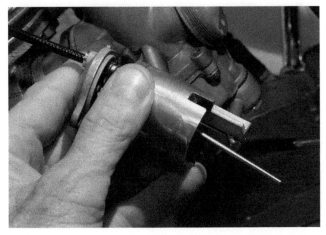

The carburetor top is almost there. Next Garry sets the return spring in and puts the throttle cable into the valve.

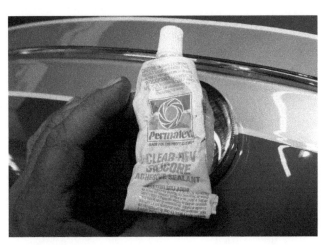

Clear silicone is our adhesive of choice for attaching the glue-on knee pads.

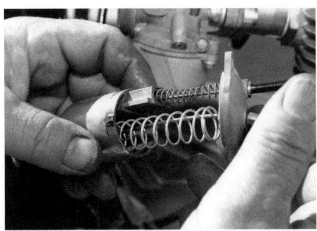

Garry checks the fit of the guide sleeve and spring inside the air slide. Nice fit, the assembly is moving freely.

Here you can see how we've spread it evenly across the back side of the knee pad.

We put just a light coat of silicone on the back of the knee-grip. Use a light coat to prevent a mess.

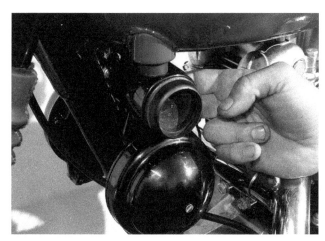

Reflector bracket is mounted under the tank, secured by a spigot, rubber cup, and self-locking nut.

Garry lowers the gas tank in place slowly, making sure the coils and wiring are in the right place. Keeping his right hand on the front of the gas tank, protecting it from chipping on the top lug.

After tightening the tank down and making sure the reflector bracket is straight, the amber reflector is set into the rubber and held on by the chrome ring.

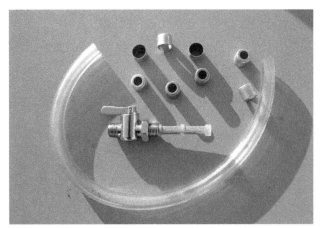

Here we have the petrol pipe and ferrules. Don't worry, the taps were later replaced with originals. The re-pops like this, are one thing you can spot on an OK restoration.

The bike was missing its toolbox side panel. We had a good used original. Next the panel knob clip will be riveted in place, some light oil or soapy water will help the grommets slide into place.

We are pretty much done with most of the rebuild. Here I stuff a rag into the oil tank prior to trimming off some paint around the top so the filler cap can go on. Nice paint, thanks Shadley Bros.

Most restorations look good at twenty feet. The difference between some of those and the example seen here is in the little things. This one looks as good at two feet as it does at twenty. Like any other type of craftsmanship, the difference is in the details.

Chapter Three

Keep 'em Running

There's Nothing Like the Sound of a Triumph

Most of this chapter is compliments of Mitch Klempf, the man who for nearly 30 years has run Klempf's British Parts near Rochester, Minnesota. In addition to selling British parts, Klempf has ridden, repaired and road raced a variety of Triumphs. So we decided to ask Mitch just what it takes to keep one of the old twins running on a regular basis. Though they look great sitting in a place of honor in your office (speaking from experience here) they look (and

Keeping them running can be challenging. The pre-unit bikes like this UK-spec '62 Bonnie are more mechanically complex, and also harder to find parts for, than the later unit bikes.

sound) way better going down the road. These are motorcycles, meant to be ridden daily not dusted weekly.

Q&A, MITCH KLEMPF

Mitch, start by telling us how you started in the British bike parts business?

I started out riding a small Honda as a kid. When I wanted something bigger I looked at the 305 Honda, but I also looked at the 1964 Bonneville. The Bonnie looked pretty good, better than the 305 Honda. In those days, you couldn't get parts, the dealers weren't very good and they didn't want to stock any parts. So I started keeping some extra parts, then other people began to call me when the dealer didn't have something. And the business grew out of that.

Tell me about the business today?

Well, It's mostly my wife and me and one employee. We sell parts for Triumph, BSA and Norton. Recently we bought out Moores Cycle Supply, so it's a lot busier. With the Triumphs we try to have parts for all the vintage bikes, we don't have parts for the newer, Hinckley bikes.

Is it harder to sell parts for older machines, as opposed to something newer?

Yes, we have trouble because people don't know what they have, and they always say "it's never been apart." So we send them standard rings for example,

Mitch Klempf in the warehouse with the Rob North framed triple he road raced for many years. " I could usually beat supposedly faster and newer bikes," recalls Mitch. "They might have more horsepower than me and be faster on the straight, but I could usually get ahead, and stay ahead, in the corners."

The warehouses are impressive, the parts include NOS, re-pop and used. Much of the stock comes from other dealers and parts outlets that have gone out of business.

The person who answers the phone is likely to be Mitch himself. He keeps notes on each call in case there's a question later.

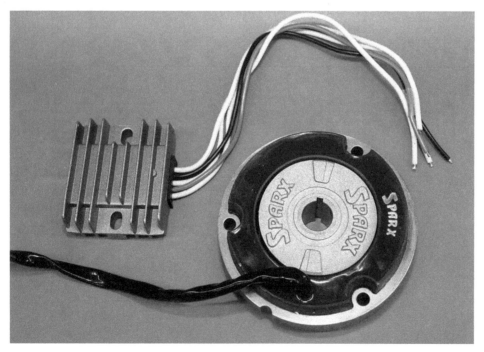

The Sparx alternator kit is produced overseas, is rated at 180 to 200 watts, and comes with rotor and electronic regulator.

and it turns out the cylinders are forty-over. If they would measure things and not assume so much it would be easier to send the right parts.

So many of these bikes end up just sitting in a garage or a museum. Can a Triumph twin be used as a daily rider, or at least for basic transportation? And what are the issues that arise when you try to use them daily?

Yes, any of the bikes from the '60s can be used on a regular basis, and we have customers that use them in this way. There are some problems that crop up though.

How do you categorize the issues that come up when these bikes are run daily and how can they be overcome?

The biggest problems break down into three areas: the charging circuit, the points ignition, and the carburetors. And then there are a few additional areas people should watch out for. Each one of these really deserves it's own discussion.

CHARGING CIRCUIT

The alternator output is too low. These bikes never did charge very well, they were only 120 watt alternators originally. With the headlight and taillight on that only leaves a few amps left for charging the battery, and only when you're running at 3,000 rpm or higher. At idle you are running a negative charge, you're taking power out of the battery.

Let's say you are riding in town with lights on and using the blinkers, you aren't charging the battery. In the old days we never ran with the lights on during the day so even if it discharged a little at night, we at least had a fully charged battery when we turned on the lights. The other charging circuit problem we see is rotors that have lost magnetism, so the output drops. Twenty years ago you never heard about it, but some of those have lost 20 to 30 percent of their output. You also have to watch the old rotors because sometimes the center section comes loose from the rest of the rotor.

Installing a high output alternator helps. The new ones are 180 to 200 watts. And most of these are 3-phase alternators so they put out a higher percentage of their maximum output at a much lower rpm. Currently we have original and reproduction systems from Lucas and the orient.

The new solid state regulators are great too. They eliminate the rectifier and diodes. The rectifier was a lot of trouble because the center mounting bolt also mounts one of the diodes, when you tighten up the bolt the diode wants to rotate which breaks the internal connection.

The Lucas alternator kit is available at Mitch's and comes with stator, rotor, diodes and rectifier.

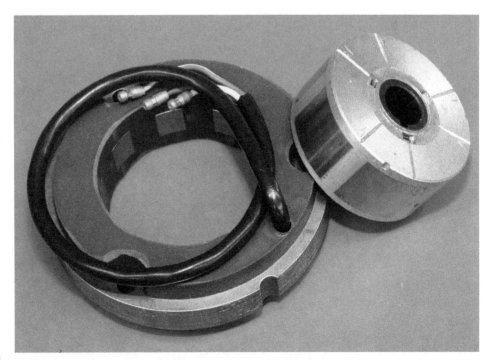

It's a good idea to buy your alternator as a kit, as shown, with both stator and rotor.

Per Mitch's warning, you have to be careful when mounting the traditional rectifier.

I recommend a new three-phase alternator and rotor, in the highest output you can get, it's still marginal by modern standards, but it's a lot better than what they came with new. Installing these takes a little care, it's not just plug and play, that's why we send along an extra set of instructions.

ELECTRONIC IGNITION

Electronic ignition is good, they put out more spark than a set of points and eliminate the maintenance associated with points. They draw more power than points however, so if there was a charging issue before, it gets worse after you add the electronic ignition.

What we encounter is a situation where the bike runs fine initially with the new ignition, but as the battery runs down it starts to run worse and worse, then finally quits. If you let it sit for a few hours (and it has a good battery) the battery recovers and the bike starts and the whole thing happens again. So now the customer calls and blames the ignition right away. Usually it's not the ignition, it's insufficient alternator output. Typically when an ignition goes bad they just die. People want the easy answer though and the ignition is easy to blame.

We handle Lucas-Rita, they quit making them, but we still have some in stock. We also handle

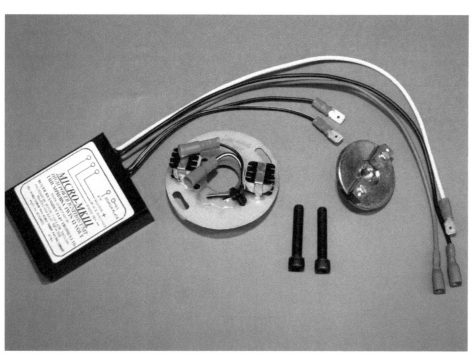

The well-known Boyer ignition assembly comes complete with the pickup plate, rotor and electronic control unit, and even includes two possible rotor-mounting bolts (British or US thread).

Boyer, Tri-Spark and Sparx. Tri-Spark says their unit draws less power than the others but I haven't tested one. The Lucas ignitions work good, in spite of Lucas' Prince-of-Darkness reputation. Most of these ignitions have a set advance curve, they aren't user-changeable like some of the aftermarket Harley ignitions.

WIRING ISSUES

Wiring can be an issue, the harnesses are old and the vibration creates problems. Sometimes the owners route the harness wrong so the wires rub on one spot and wear through. Fuses are also a problem. The original main fuse was marked "35," but it was actually 17 amps continuous and 35 amps for a surge. When someone blows that fuse they put in a 35 amp car fuse, so it's really too much current and then they melt the harness. And people hook the batteries up backwards, they hook it up negative ground and there go your diodes and maybe the whole harness.

AMALS SUCK?

Amals aren't such a bad carburetor, I think they got a bum wrap. They wore out, but that was really about the only real problem. Now people don't wear them out like they did before, because they don't drive as far or as often. Most of the problems we see are

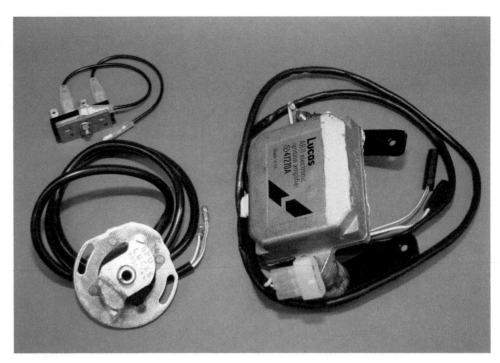

The Lucas-Rita ignition is out of production but still available at Mitch's shop.

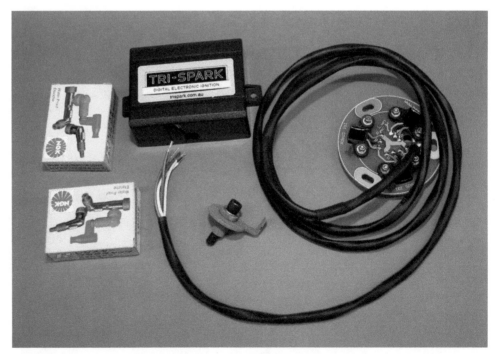

Despite the name, Tri-Spark makes electronic ignition units for both twins and triples (triple unit shown) and comes as a complete kit.

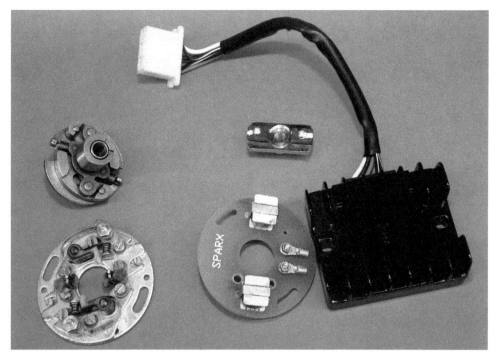

Contrast. On the left, a stock points ignition assembly with advance unit. On the right, a complete electronic ignition unit from Sparx.

caused by the owner. The slides stick because people over-torque the flange nuts, and warp the body. That happens whether the carb is old or new. The other big thing comes when you leave gas in the carbs during storage. The problem is especially bad with this new gas, it doesn't stay fresh very long.

If you leave fuel in the carbs over the winter it plugs up the idle circuits and the bike runs poorly. Water in the gas makes it worse, then it forms this white chalky stuff. That chalky material gets hard when it dries and you can't blow it out of the idle circuits, you really have to replace the carb body. The later Amals have drains in the bowls, you should drain it once a month or anytime the bike will sit for more than a month. Also after washing the bike or riding in a big rain storm.

PETCOCKS

Petcocks have troubles too. Some don't shut off, so they continue to drip into the carb and fuel eventually collects in the bottom of the motor. Now the stator, which is wrapped in a plastic type material, balloons out and wrecks the alternator.

The problem with petcocks is there are so many styles. I ask people, 'do you want one that works or one that looks like the old one?' You

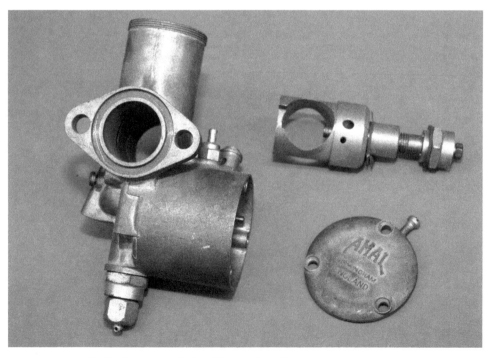

Parts are available for most of the old Amal carburetors, even the monobloc models.

can't get a good one unless you're willing to accept a slightly different style. The ones that we hesitate to sell do not come with a warranty. So If you buy those and they leak you are stuck with them.

Nuts 'n Bolts

People call the bolts 'Whitworth,' but most of the fasteners used on Triumphs are actually Cycle Engineering Institute. The Brits had their own system, they were all 26 threads per inch regardless of bolt diameter.

In 1969 they started to change but they didn't change everything, a few things changed earlier than that, as early as 1967, but 1969 was the big year for the change-over to what we call American or SAE threads.

People use the wrong bolts all the time. With some there is only a two-thread per inch difference. For example, a 1/4-26 is British, a 1/4 - 28 is American fine thread. The other one that's really close is 5/16 inch. The English bolt is 26 threads per inch, the American fine thread is 24 threads per inch.

You have to remember, the bikes are getting old, parts are getting swapped, people say the bike wasn't taken apart before, but the machine is 40 years old. Guys buy stuff on the internet so

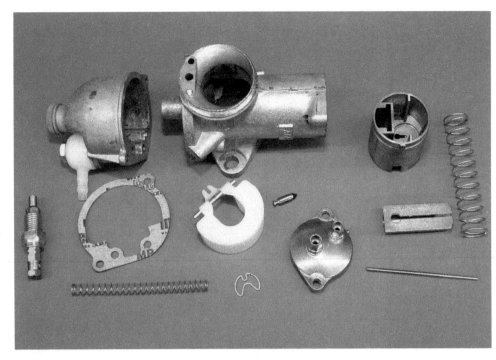

The newer concentric model carburetors can be replaced as a complete unit or you can buy most of the parts individually.

Newer float bowls, as shown, generally have a drain plug. This way it's easy to drain the gas at the start of a storage period.

Used on some of the latest vintage Triumphs, the Mark II carbs are likewise available as complete units or you can purchase individual components. At Klempf's you can even buy Bing carburetors used on just a few Triumph models.

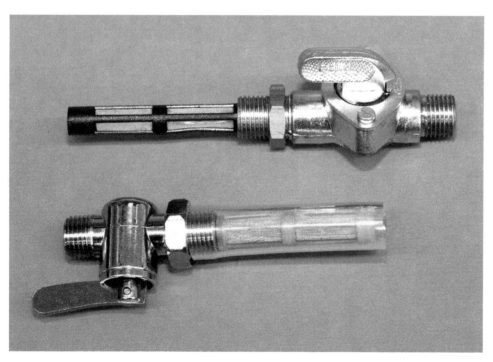

These are the two most common petcocks sold at Klempf's. The upper one, which is not a perfect reproduction, is by far the most dependable model currently being sold.

they don't know what they are getting, a lot of the guys don't really know what they have. If they tell me the thread per inch of a particular bolt I can tell them if it's the right one or not and sell them the correct one.

GEARING AND TRANSMISSIONS

If you want a higher final gear so the bikes will work better on the highway, you can change one of the sprockets, but you can only go so far. People ask if you can put a five speed in a four-speed case, and the answer is yes, you can (even a pre-unit). It takes a good mechanic to do this, though, because the quadrant and the plunger are different.

The five-speeds shift better and the ratios are spaced out better. High gear though is still one-to-one, but you could raise the overall gearing and then install a five-speed. Remember, the early five-speeds from 1971, 1972, and early 1973, were weak so you don't want one of those.

Most of the bikes sit so much that sometimes the clutch plates stick together. Then guys just put the front wheel up against the building, start the engine and dump it into gear, which often destroys the transmission and the case. The better way to do it is to take the clutch apart and pry each plate off from the one next to it.

Overflowing Oil and a General Attitude

With some of these old bikes, when they sit, oil can work it's way from the tank, through the oil pump and end up in the engine's sump. If they check the oil and find it's way low, they add oil. Now the bike is over-filled and when you kick it to life it starts smoking and may blow out the seals. We tell riders to check the oil when they come back from a ride, then check it again when they leave on the next ride. If there's a big difference it's all in the sump.

These old bikes need to be used more, sitting isn't good for them. When people do ride them though, they have to do the maintenance: Tighten the chain, adjust the valves, check and tighten all the bolts.

You can't expect an old Triumph to run as well as the new bikes. You can't ride a twin as hard as your buddy does his new Harley, they just weren't designed for it. They're not meant to run 80 and 90 all day. The triples are better, they will run really hard all day but they still need more maintenance than a modern bike. Whether it's a twin or a triple, this is old technology, you have to understand the machine and be willing to do some maintenance and TLC.

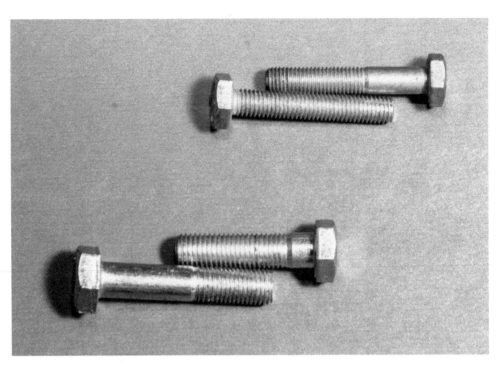

Here we have SAE bolts next to CEI, 1/4 inch (upper) and 5/16 (lower). In both cases the SAE bolt is on top. The significant thing is how close these are which means it's really easy to put the wrong bolt in the wrong hole and bugger up the threads. Most tap and die sets have thread pitch gauges which makes it easy to identify the number of threads per inch.

When picking fasteners, pay attention to the markings on the head. Quality SAE bolts have the typical three or six dash markings indicating Grade 5 or 8, while the CEI have a set of markings all their own.

Chapter Four

Disassemble The Engine

The '69 Engine Gets Stripped Down

When it comes to taking an engine apart, remember to take your time and keep the parts organized. If a part won't come off, ask yourself why before you get out the hammer. Check the manual, think your way through the problem. Inspect the parts as you take them apart. Cardboard boxes and clear plastic bags make a good way to keep them in logical groupings. Make notes as you pull the parts off, as to which look worn or questionable, and take some digital photos. Do another careful inspection as you clean all the parts in solvent.

Extra time taken during disassembly will pay big dividends when it comes time to put it all back together again.

A beautiful thing, a recently rebuilt 1969 T120 motor.

1969 bottom end motor ready to be disassembled.

The rotor nut is removed, then the rotor and stator.

The clutch hub is being removed using a clutch hub extractor.

A view prior to the removal of the pinion gears.

Using a hammer and punch, the tab washer is peeled back from the rotor.

The timing gears are removed using an extractor or puller.

Now, using an extractor, the timing pinion is removed.

The counter shaft sprocket gear is removed next.

The cover plate is heated prior to removal, don't over-do the heat.

The case is heated so the cylinder studs can be removed.

The primary side is now completely disassembled.

The transmission level plug is removed now.

With the cover off, the transmission gears are removed...top and bottom, the mainshaft and layshaft gears.

The high gear bearing boss is also heated for removal.

Then we split the cases, and then the crankshaft assembly is removed as shown.

Next, heat is applied to the right side engine case to ease removal of the main bearing.

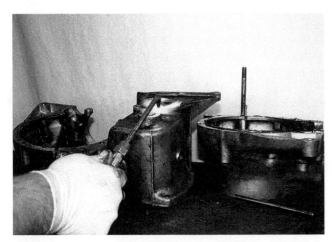

The case surrounding the low gear bushings is heated so the bushing can be removed.

The inner transmission cover prior to disassembly.

Chapter Five

The Engine Assembly

The '69 Engine Goes Together

The engine assembly seen here is the work of Garry Chitwood. As the builder of many Triumph engines, Garry has some advice for anyone who wants to undertake their first engine overhaul.

First, Garry feels that this is a do-able deal, "for anyone with some mechanical experience."

Garry goes on to explain that, "the pictures show a lot of detail and it's our intent that the average builder working at home should be able to do the same thing seen here with only common mechanic's tools and a few special Triumph tools. They probably want to have a service manual in addi-

A nearly finished '69 Bonneville, with a recently rebuilt 650cc engine.

tion to this book, that way they would be sure to have any torque or clearance specifications that we didn't include.

If you ask Garry what's the one important thing about rebuilding an engine that needs to be kept in mind, he says that it's cleanliness. "I can't say enough about keeping everything clean," explains Garry. "That motor should go back together as clean as it could ever be. I like to lay everything out on a clean table covered with paper towels. I inspect the parts as I take the engine apart, and then I inspect them again after they've been cleaned. A lot of times, when you inspect them a second time after they've been cleaned, you can then see wear you might have missed on the first inspection, like on the gears or shafts or maybe the cylinders.

According to Garry, the mistakes that people make are the big obvious ones, like putting the crank in the wrong case half. A more common mistake is to break a piston ring as the cylinder is pushed down over the pistons. "Installing the cylinder over the pistons is very tedious," explains Garry, "you have to take time so you avoid breaking any rings. When I assemble an engine, I'm constantly turning it over. Every time I put another part of it together I make sure the engine rotates and isn't binding. And after I have the cylinders pushed down onto the case halves I turn the engine over again so I know there isn't a piston ring jammed in the cylinder. Before the assembly I like to be sure the bores were cut correctly and that there's at least .0045 inches of clearance between the piston skirt and the cylinder. I've seem them both ways, too loose and the pistons slap, too tight and you might seize the motor.

And be sure to wash the cylinders in hot soapy water before putting them back on the motor, because the water will clean the walls of any debris that might be there. Any metal filings left from boring or honing will be flushed out. Then the cylinders should be wiped down with clean oil so you're sure there's oil on those cylinder walls when the engine first fires. Assuming the motor starts and runs, you need to do the first oil change after only 500 or 600 miles.

First we removed the flywheel bolt from the crank.

Garry is using a screw-drive attachment for the 3/8 inch ratchet to remove the sludge trap screw.

An old spoke bent to have a hook at the end is used to removed the sludge trap tube.

They don't come out easily, a punch and adjustable wrench are used to twist and help pull out the sludge trap tube.

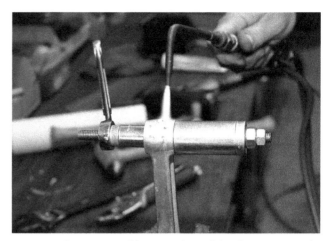

Here, we're using a blow torch and bushing removal tool to pull the top connecting rod bushing.

Here it is, the old sludge trap tube.

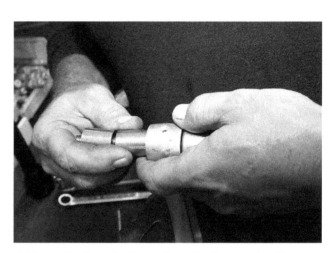

Using a bush tool, Garry installs the new bushing.

Garry cleans the crank with parts-wash solvent, and uses compressed air to ensure the oil galleries are open.

Here you can see the new bushing being install in the connecting rod.

A red Scotch-brite pad is used as shown to polish the new bushing.

The new top end bushings don't come with oil holes so Garry has to create one. Note the bolt used to ensure the drill bit doesn't drop through and scar the bottom of the new bushing.

Now Garry can check the wrist pin to bushing clearance. Clearance should be .06885 inches.

A red Scotch-brite pad is also used to polish the journals, which were in pretty good condition when the motor was disassembled.

This shows the clean sludge trap tube and crank plug screw prior to reassembly.

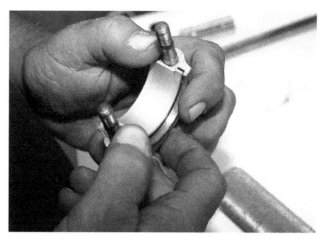

Here the bearing is snapped into the upper half of the connecting rod. Note the locating tab.

Garry is installing the sludge trap tube and showing how the flywheel bolt holds the sludge trap in place.

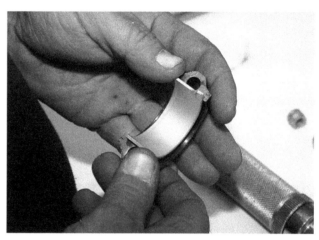

Next, the rod bearing is slipped into the bottom half, or cap, of the connecting rod.

Garry polishes the connecting rod with a red Scotch-brite pad before he installs the big end bearing. You don't want any nicks or raised areas.

Before assembly the parts are all pre-lubed with clean oil.

Now it's time to put the cap on the connecting rods, these caps have to go on the same connecting rod, in the same position, as when they were disassembled.

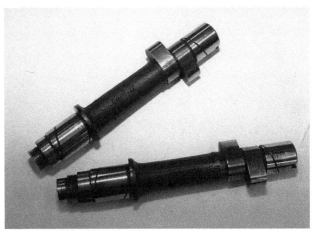

Shown here are two cams, intake and exhaust, for our 1969 Bonneville. The exhaust cam is dished out at the end and has a pin for the advance.

Once the cap is on Garry can screw on the nuts that hold it all together.

The pinion gears for intake and exhaust are interchangeable.

The connecting rods are installed to the crank. The nuts are torqued to 28 ft. lbs.

With fresh oil on the bearing surface, Garry installs the intake cam to the timing side chest.

Shown here is the key being installed on the intake cam.

Garry and Ryan install the pinion gear to the intake cam shaft using a socket as a driver and brass hammer.

A hammer and punch are used to fully seat the key in the cam shaft.

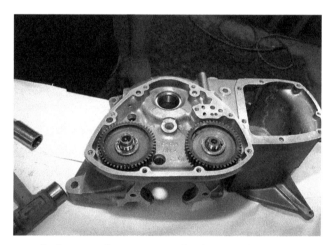

Here's the complete timing side chest with pinion gears and cams.

Now the intake cam can be lined up with the pinion gear. The timing mark should line up with keyway on the cam.

Now it's time to install the high gear bearing and ring clip in the drive-side case.

1. Next on the installation list is the high gear seal on the timing chest side.

3. Garry uses a brass drift and hammer to install the lay shaft bearing.

2. Garry is setting up lay shaft bearing outside of the transmission housing. The cup he's holding contains the needle bearings for the bottom lay shaft.

4. Shown on the right is high gear, a gear box sprocket, lock washer and nut.

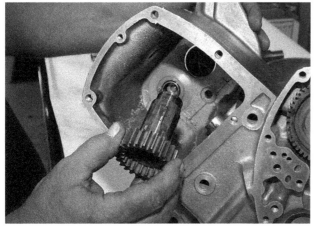

Garry is installing the high gear in the timing side chest.

Now comes the washer and nut.

Here you see the high gear installed through the transmission case.

A channel lock and adjustable wrench are used to hold the sprocket and tighten the lock nut.

Next, the sprocket gear is set onto the high gear shaft.

After being tightened, the aluminum washer is bent over to lock the nut in place.

1. Time now to put the breather hose in the drive side case.

3. Garry and Ryan finish installing the complete crank assembly in the drive side case.

2. Here you see Garry and Ryan installing the complete crank assembly in the drive side case.

4. We use Honda Bond (gasket sealer) for the crank cases. A thin layer is spread evenly over both case halves before they're bolted together.

At this point the timing side case is dropped onto the other case half.

Shown here are the two complete cases joined together.

A rubber mallet is used to ensure the two case halves butt up together. Garry just taps the case gently until the case halves are lined up and butted together.

Shown here are the intermediate gear, timing pinion gear and spacer with key.

Now it's starting to look like an engine.

Here you can see the timing pinion installed with the key and spacer.

Garry installs the spindle for the intermediate wheel.

This is the oil pump and hardware laid out and ready to be installed.

This is a view of a complete timing gear assembly with the intermediate and crank gear. The timing marks are correct as shown.

Garry is installing the oil pump to the pinion gear intake cam. Inset photo shows the drive for the oil pump.

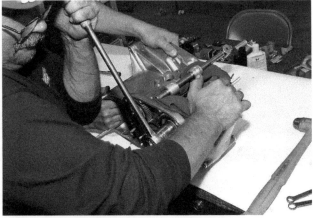

While Ryan holds the engine, Garry tightens down the timing gear nuts to between 30 and 40 ft. lbs.

Here's a view of the complete assembled timing gears and oil pump. The large O-ring ensures that the gears don't slip out of place as the engine is moved around, and will come off before the cover goes on.

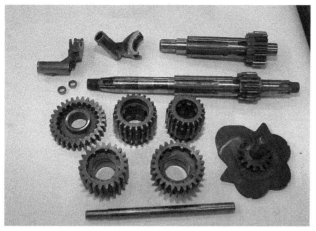

This is a view of the transmission parts before assembly.

Next, Garry installs the gear selector cam plate.

The parts are combined into the assembly as shown, before installation in the case.

Now the complete transmission gearset can be installed into the case.

Garry is putting in the lay shaft thrust washer. The hole in the thrust washer goes up against the pin seen on the inside of the case.

Shown here is the complete transmission with the gearset and gear selector cam plate in position.

This is the index plunger for the gear selector cam plate installed in the transmission.

Garry is holding the index plunger for the gear selector cam plate.

Here Garry is pointing out the gear selector cam plate.

Shown here is the inner transmission cam plate, operating quadrant, lay shaft bearing, main shaft bearing, and circlip.

TRIUMPH'S ANTIQUE FOUR-SPEED TRANSMISSION

Four-speed transmissions have become antiques in our modern world. Most modern vehicles, from the truck in the driveway to the new motorcycle in the garage, have at least five gears. Yet, people in the know say the old Triumph four-speed transmission is a good durable unit. "Those four-speeds are more reliable than later five speed transmissions," according to Garry Chitwood, "and they stand up to abuse well. Back in my younger days I definitively gave them some abuse, but I never did break one."

The other really nice thing about the Triumph four-speed transmission is ease of service. "It's a very straight forward piece to take

Garry heats the inner transmission cover for easy installation of the main shaft bearing.

Here the split pin is installed as shown.

After installing the bearing, Garry installs the circlip for the main shaft bearing.

All the components are installed in the transmission housing. Time to install the gasket...

Now the quadrant spindle is installed into the transmission inner cover.

...and the inner transmission cover, which is tapped carefully until it seats up against the gasket.

apart, inspect and put back together," says resident expert Chitwood. "The shift forks are numbered and you should put those back where they came out, but otherwise the transmission is easy to reassemble. While the old Harley four-speed used shims and required careful set up, the Triumph transmission requires only common sense and careful assembly of all the parts. During assembly, you can either put the gears on the lay shaft one gear at a time, working in the case. Or you can assembled the whole thing outside the case, as I did, and then just slide the whole assembly back into the case."

All the parts need to be inspected when the transmission is apart, but there isn't any one gear or bearing that's more prone to wear than another. "The older pre-unit transmissions used brass bushings to support the shafts," says Garry. "But by about '62 or '63 they all used needle bearings. The old brass bushing were a pain in the ass, but the needle bearings almost never wear out."

If anything does wear out in your four-speed unit-style transmission, parts are easy to find. From bearings to shift forks, and gears to gaskets, everything can be purchased from any good Triumph parts source.

Garry says there are no particular tricks to assembling the four-speed transmissions, though he does like to rotate the gears as he's doing the assembling to ensure nothing is binding, much as he does when assembling the engine. For lubricant, Garry likes the Lucas products, and is careful to coat everything with the heavy gear oil during assembly "that oil helps to hold all the part together and in place during assembly, " says Garry, "but really you could use any good 80/90 gear oil in the transmission.

Garry shows the cam plate operating quadrant in the middle notch position before the inner cover is completely sealed.

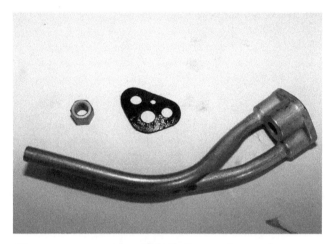

Here you can see the oil feed pipe, gasket and nut.

Here Garry is installing the oil feed pipe on the engine.

Shown here are all of the parts needed for the primary side of the engine.

Here's the installation of the engine sprocket seal to the primary side of the engine.

Here is the primary side of our 1969 Bonneville engine without the clutch assembly or primary drive.

Shown here is the sprocket seal installed. Above it you can see the sprocket/primary-chain oiler, make sure there is no interference between the oiler and the chain or sprocket.

First we install the cover plate with oil seal to the primary side of the engine.

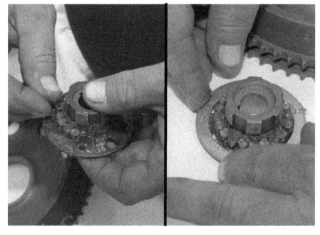

Garry pre-assembles the roller bearing on the clutch hub, as shown, then drops on the thrust washer.

Now the clutch hub basket can be slipped over the clutch-hub roller bearing.

Shown here is the key installed on the main shaft.

Next, the screw pins are installed in the center hub.

Shown here is the three alternator studs already installed into the primary side of the engine.

Shown here is the completed clutch basket assembly.

Here we're installing the primary blade tensioner.

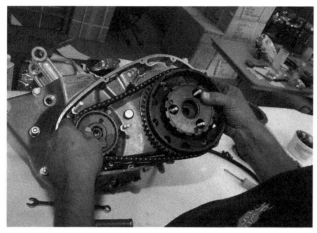

The primary drive is assembled as shown and then slipped over the pinion and transmission shafts.

The washer is the first step in installing the ratchet gear assembly. Inset shows sleeve in place on the shaft.

Here you can see how the blade tensioner is adjusted to take the slack out of the primary chain.

Next on the list is the spring for the ratchet gear assembly.

Shown is the complete ratchet gear assembly. Note, Though it might seem confusing, Garry Chitwood switches from side to side when assembling an engine, and that's how the assembly is presented here.

Now comes the kick-start pinion.

1. Now I install the kick starter ratchet gear.

3. Garry is folding over the tab washer to the nut.

2. Once the lock washer is in place Garry installs the nut for the ratchet gear assembly.

Garry shows a sleeve nut for the alternator wires.

Here we start with the first bonded clutch plate. There are six steel plates and six bonded plates in all.

79

Shown here is the stator, rotor and pressure plate assembly.

Shown here is the complete primary assembly with clutch basket, stator and rotor.

Now we install the rotor on the primary side of the engine.

Shown here is the complete pressure plate, clutch spring and nut. Adjustment is discussed on page 82.

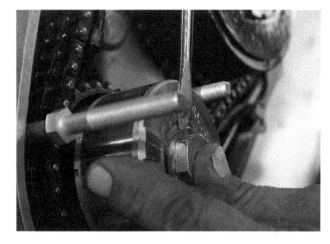

Once the nut is tightened to 20 to 25 ft. lbs., you need to bend over the rotor tab washer onto the rotor nut.

Time now to install the cylinder studs to the crank case. Gary puts a little red Loctite on the threads before tightening them down into the case.

Shown here is the cylinder, pistons, rings, tappet guide blocks, lifters and base gasket.

Here you can see how we install the lifters into the tappet guide block.

Here's the guide block and lifters.

Before installing the new pistons, the circlip is inserted in one side.

The guide block is ready to be installed in the cylinder. One is intake and one is exhaust. On the later bikes the exhaust guide block has two little oil passages to keep the tappets lubricated.

After coating the pin with oil, the piston pin is slipped through the piston, connecting rod and into the other side of the piston.

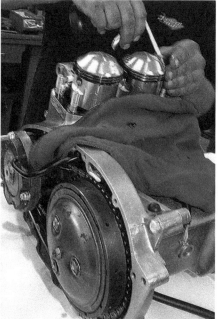

Here you can see Garry carefully installing the rings on the pistons. You have to be careful, it's easy to break a ring.

Garry is using the oil can to lube the pistons before he installs them into the cylinder.

This is a two-man operation: Ryan holds the cylinder above the pistons while Garry slips them up into the cylinder.

THE CLUTCH

Like the four-speed transmission, the clutch assembly used on the unit (650cc) Triumph is durable and easy to service. All the units in question use a clutch with 6 bonded plates and all use 30 weight oil in the primary side. Unlike some motorcycle clutches that require the bonded plates to be soaked before installation, Garry simply recommends putting a liberal coating of 30w oil on both the steel and bonded plates as they are set into the clutch hub.

Assembling the clutch requires two adjustments: the threaded tension adjusters, and the initial clutch free play. Garry likes to set the threaded tension adjusters flush with the studs as shown, but warns that you have to pay attention once the bike is started. "If there's any clutch slippage at all once the bike is on the road, give the adjusters an additional half turn."

The initial free play is adjusted with the central threaded adjuster and lock nut. With the transmission assembled and the clutch cable disconnected, the adjuster is screwed in until it just touches the pushrod (located inside the mainshaft), then unscrewed one-half turn and locked in place with the lock nut. Once the bike is assembled the lever free-play can be adjusted with the threaded collar on the lever assembly.

As we said, the clutch used on these bikes is a very durable unit, but that doesn't mean they didn't burn up occasionally. "You have to keep the primary chain adjusted with a good tensioner blade," warns Garry Chitwood. "The other thing you have to be careful with is the oil level, that's where people have trouble. They let it get low and the next thing you know they start burning up clutches. You can tell because when you put it in gear it wants to creep forward even with the clutch lever pulled all the way back. People aren't careful enough about checking the oil level on the primary side of the bike."

Installing the pistons requires patience, Garry squeezes the rings together and gently works the piston up into the cylinder. Ring compressors are available, but Gary prefers this old skool method.

Shown here is the complete bottom end and installed cylinder.

After the pistons are pushed up into the cylinders, Garry slides the cylinder down onto the block. A metal strap is placed under the pistons to keep them from moving as the cylinder is pushed down.

These are all of the parts of the oil-relief valve.

The guide block and tappets were installed into the cylinder before it was installed on the cases.

This is the oil relief valve just before it's installed into the piston.

Now we can install the primary cover and gasket. The access hole allows for clutch pushrod adjustment without removing the cover.

Here is a valve and valve grinding compound, Garry likes to lap in the valves before final assembly.

Next, Garry installs the timing chest cover and gasket.

Garry puts compound on the valve face and then spins the valve with an electric drill.

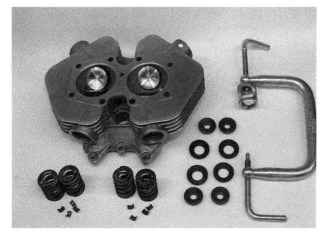

Shown here is the cylinder head and complete spring kit.

Here we're installing and compressing the valve spring...

Shown here is the outer transmission cover with all of the parts.

Shown here is the inner transmission cover.

...once the new valve spring is compressed, Garry installs the split valve keepers.

Shown here is the complete gear change quadrant, plunger installed.

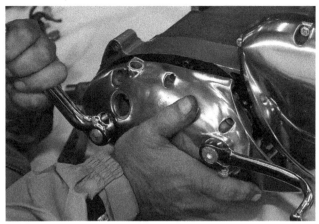

1) The outer transmission is completely assembled, now we can push it into position. There is a stop on the inner cover, Garry is pulling back on the kick start lever so it goes over the stop.

2) Garry does the final tightening of the transmission cover screws. Hammer blows keep the screwdriver seated in the screw as he turns the handle.

5) Now we install the cylinder head.

3) Pushrod tubes are next. Here we're installing the bottom metal ring for the oil seal.

4) The pushrod tubes are already installed over the tappet guide blocks.

Garry has the cylinder head in place and torques the cylinder head bolts down to 18 to 20 ft. lbs.

Now we add the drive gear to the tack-drive unit.

Here we are installing the intake spigot on the cylinder head.

Here Garry is holding the gear box body and gear housing.

Garry is about to install the securing screw into the gear box body, part of the tach-drive assembly.

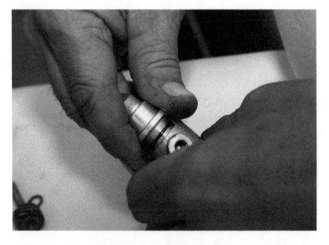

The gear housing can now be installed into the gear box body.

1) Now the set screw can be installed into the complete tach-drive gear box.

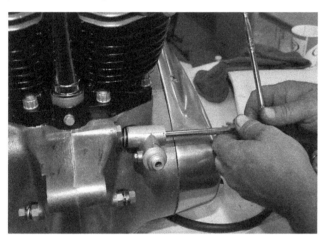

3) Now Garry can install the gear box to the right side crank case.

2) Garry holds the securing screw and installs the sealing washer.

4) The gear box body has been tightened and Garry can now install the driving gear.

Here's the oil sending unit installed in the timing cover.

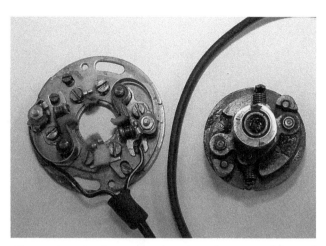

Shown here is the contact breaker plate assembly and the auto-advance unit.

We have a new patent plate and drive screws for the timing chest cover.

A completed timing chest with breaker plate and advance unit.

A few blows from a small hammer are all that's required to install the screws.

A finished 1969 T120 Bonneville engine in the frame.

Chapter Six

Gallery

A Visual Guide to Restoration

There's that old cliche', a picture is worth a thousand words. Whether it's strictly true or not, we've chosen to provide you with high quality photos of the significant models manufactured by Triumph from the period 1959 to 1970, with only a brief and precise description of each model and year, provided by Triumph expert, Lindsay Brooke. We present these as very accurate restorations, they are not perfect. There may be no perfect restorations as some things are open to interpretation. Also, remember that colors are affected not only by the photographer's equipment and time of day, but also the processing, and finally, the printing. If nothing else, this is a group of really, really nice old motorcycles.

Perhaps not what we think of when we think of a Triumph Bonneville, the 1959 models did, however, come with the right equipment under the hood - a 650cc engine with two! carburetors.

The iconic T120 Bonneville 650cc sports twin launched in September, 1958 with engine serial number 020377. Its splayed-port cylinder head mounted twin, unfiltered 1 1/16-in. Amal 376/204 Monobloc carburetors. Lacking integral float bowls, the so-called "chopped" Monoblocs were fed by a separate Amal GP-type rubber-mounted fuel chamber.

U.S. market Bonnies came with the 3-1/4-gal. TR6 fuel tank while U.K. machines had a 4-1/2-gallon tank, both were finished in Tangerine and Pearl Grey colors. Early U.K. and general export Bonnie oil tanks were sprayed in black, later changed to Pearl Grey. Gearboxes on T120 models used the Slick Shift-type outer cover, but without that unit's actuator mechanism inside.

U.S. market 1959 TR6 Trophy models offered in both low-pipe TR6/A and high-pipe TR6/B continued in the previous year's Aztec Red and Ivory paint scheme, but with the white on top. New for the year were a larger capacity (1-gal.) oil tank, one-piece forged crankshaft, and 8.5:1 pistons with stouter crown and reprofiled skirt.

Like the Bonneville, the Trophy 650s featured a Lucas K2FC "red label" competition magneto. Smiths chronometric tachometers were standard on the /A models, optional on the /Bs. The larger twinseat from the 500cc Tiger made its way onto the Trophy this year, complete with a white-piping border.

Triumph totally revamped the Bonnie's styling for 1960, transforming it into the sporty-looking "twin-carb Trophy." They also gave it a new model code—TR7/A and /B. The headlamp nacelle was replaced by a separate Lucas unit, and the valenced fenders were swapped for leaner Trophy items. The low bars on this example are U.K.-market, and the air-filter canisters are incorrect.

Triumph's twin-downtube duplex frame was big news on the 650cc model range for 1960. U.S. Bonnies got a standard tachometer (and special tach-drive timing cover). The "chopped" Monoblocs and central fuel bowl remained through 1960. The folding kickstart lever on this bike was not standard on Bonnies until the following year.

'60 TR6

Use in U.S. off-road racing quickly showed up a major design flaw of Triumph's new duplex frame—its lack of a lower rail to brace the gas tank and reinforce the steering head area. Triumph responded in 1960 with a new front frame section incorporating a lower tank rail. And though popular with some restorers, the Made in England transfer did not appear on Triumph 650 downtubes until 1971.

For 1960, Triumph's 650s traded their front-mounted generators for a Lucas alternator mounted on the drive side of the crankshaft, which meant a new primary cover. Also new for all 650s was the front fork with two-way damping. The road-going Trophy's 3.25 x 19-inch ribbed front tire and 4.00 x 18-inch universal rear were shared with the year's Bonnie.

'61 T120C

1961 TRI. T120

Further chassis changes for the 1961 model year included an even steeper steering head angle and a revised gas-tank retainer strap. Two U.S. market fuel tanks were available—the 3-gal. variant (shown) joined by a new 5-gal. vessel. Some U.S.-market Triumphs still were fitted with U.K.-market front registration blades, the front fenders of others had the the holes closed with plugs.

1961 TRI. T120

Monobloc carbs with full float chambers became standard on Bonnies early in the 1961 model year. The flamboyant medium-blue paint on the upper flank of this rare T120C's tank appears similar to 1965's Pacific Blue, but is incorrect for 1961 Bonnies which wore Triumph's robin-egg Sky Blue with the silver lower half.

The new two-tone seat with grey top, black sides, and grey lower trim made its appearance on Triumph's 1962 model range. In the engine department, Bonnies received the "waterproof" Wader version of the Lucas K2FC magneto with auto-advance.

Flamboyant (candy) Flame was the primary color of U.S. market Bonnie fuel tanks in '62. The tank's lower half, plus fenders (with Flame center stripe) were in silver. U.S. market oil tanks and tool box covers were painted black. Taillamp wiring route across and through rear fender is inelegant but correct on this restored example.

One of the great aspects of Triumph ownership is the ease in which parts can be swapped among bikes in the same model range. The 1962 TR6SS was a general-export, single-carb 650 with large touring tank, siamesed 2-into-1 roadster type (low) exhaust, and silver-painted fenders. This restored SS looks a bit more sporty wearing T120C raised exhausts and the black-upholstered seat from 1961.

High-piped 650s in 1962 came standard with engine skidplates, slimline heat shields on the exhaust headers, and block-pattern Dunlop trials tires. However, street universal tires were catalogued and were often fitted by Triumph dealers. A popular street tire for restored machines is the Dunlop K70 (shown on both ends of this restored TR6SS), once ubiquitous on British bikes.

Triumph's unit-construction 650cc engine debuted for 1963. Along with it came an all-new frame with single front downtube. Very little of the "unit" powertrain (except the 8.5:1 pistons, alloy con rods, and 1 1/16-in Amal Monobloc carbs) was directly carried over from the pre-unit era. New longer resonator-type mufflers were fitted on U.S. market machines.

The new "unit" engine finally brought coil ignition to Triumph's 650cc machines, the twin coils located under the fuel tank and the contact breaker points housed neatly underneath the chromed round cover on the new, svelte timing cover. Bonnevilles began the season without air filtration, but by year's end Triumph was fitting a new black-painted air filter housing that protected both carbs.

Advertised as the "Highway Trophy," the TR6SR in its purple-and-silver livery turned heads more than the appliance-white '63 Bonnie. This was the last year for the Smiths chronometric speedo, which accompanied a tach on the TR6SR.

The 3-1/2- gallon gas tank featured a new mounting arrangement but carried over Triumph's "mouth organ" tank badge used since 1957. The machine shown is fitted with a 1966-later type air filter canister, rather than the correct (and much thinner) 1963 item.

New stronger forks with external springs (still hidden under rubber gaitors) were a major improvement, and the primary visual difference across Triumph's 1964 twin-cylinder ranges. The correct air filter for this model year is the black-painted single canister unit. Another change for '64 was the relocation of the front footpeg mounts from lugs on the lower frame rails to the rear engine plates.

The new Smiths magnetic instruments—125-mph speedo and 10,000-rpm tach—made their Triumph debut in 1964, as did Dunlop's new K70 universal street tire (on rear wheels of Bonnies and TR6SRs). The long resonator mufflers continued as standard. On this restored example, the Triumph logo is correctly painted black and its immediate background painted gold.

"64 TR6C

The 1964-66 TR6SC was Triumph's factory "desert sled." It was a single-carb version of the Bonneville TT. The SC was offered as a west-coast model available only through Johnson Motors. Most came stripped of road equipment and TT-style upper fork shrouds without headlamp ears.

The pure off-road racing Trophy Specials came without the electrical switches on the left side panel; their mounting holes were plugged. Aluminum fenders helped save weight but the heavy metal tank badges and tank-top parcel grid did not. (Trophy buyers could order the bike without the parcel grid.) Ribbed front and universal rear tire on this restored machine are period-correct for street TR6 models.

A restored 1965 Bonnie roadster in one of Triumph's classiest paint schemes, Pacific Blue over silver. This was a year of numerous small refinements rather than major changes. One new component was the pressed-steel taillamp and license plate assembly. This was a revision of the 1964 item designed to accept the new Lucas 679 lens. This assembly was used only on 1965 models.

Front forks were also redesigned again and were phased into 1965 production part way through the '65 season. They received longer stanchions (which gave a bit more travel), and longer springs and sliders—the latter were now made from extruded steel. In a practical move, Lucas 8H horn was relocated from underneath the seat to a place underneath the gas tank ahead of the exhaust rocker box.

1965 Bonnie and Trophy dualseats gravitated between the two-tone cover shown on this restored TR6SR, and all-black upholstery. The Trophy's eye-catching Burnished Gold-over-Alaskan white paint scheme was highlighted by robin's-egg blue pinstripes separating the two colors.

A worthwhile change was the re-angled sidestand, which made it safer to park the machine on a cambered road surface without fear of tipover—but riskier to park it on the level! The attractive "Trophy Sports" decal on this bike's toolbox cover is correct for 1968 models only.

Three model years after the unit-construction engines and new chassis were introduced, Triumph brought a slew of major improvements to the 650cc range. The classic 2-1/2-gallon teardrop gas tank was introduced on U.S. versions of the Bonneville and TR6C, while their U.K. and export counter-parts retained the plumper but more practical 4-gal. tanks. Note the new "eyebrow" tank badge.

Light-grey Amal rubber handgrips were a one-year-only item on the '66 models. More importantly, the engines contained scores of modifications including a much lighter crankshaft, a new tachometer drive box, sportier camshafts and tappets, revised internal oiling, and a compression boost to 9:1. By year's end the carbs inhaled through the chromed air filter canisters shown on this restored machine.

A new-for-'66 frame was introduced for all 650cc models. It featured a relaxed 62-degree steering head angle and widened swinging arm to accommodate fatter rear rubber. Front brakes, still with only single-leading-shoe actuation, gained a 50 percent wider drum. While the machine shown has a Smiths speedometer, some 1966 TR6Cs were fitted with German-made VDO enduro instruments.

1966 was the year that much of the automobile and motorcycle industry converted to 12-volts, and Triumph was no exception. Early model-year bikes carried twin Lucas 6-volt batteries wired in series. These were replaced later by a single 12V battery. C-model 650s also gained a 6-inch headlamp. Oil tank capacity was enlarged to 3 quarts. The high-piper's fenders were polished stainless.

Looking like a million bucks in its Aubergine-and-white livery, with stainless steel fenders, the 1967 Bonnie actually was offered in three different gas-tank paint conditions, depending on date of production. The other two layouts used gold as the secondary color. Two seat conditions also appeared in '67—an all-black perch, and one with a grey top panel on the horizontal surface.

Engines received further performance upgrades, including a switch to Triumph's race-proven E3134-profile "Q" cams. Also part-way through the 1967 production run, Amal's new 30mm Concentric carburetors were introduced. The bike shown wears the Monoblocs fitted early in the season. It also has the later all-black twinseat but with the bright trim strip not used until the following year.

While it had become more of a street-scrambler by 1967, the TR6C could still kick up a mean roostertail in the dirt. The 6-inch enduro headlamps for 1966-67 came either painted or chromed. 1967 was also the year that the British bike industry began its switch from British Standard and CEI fasteners to the Unified thread forms used in the U.S. Triumph took three years to make the switch.

New exhaust systems graced the 1967 high-piped Trophies. Both pipes now exited on the left side and were silenced by a staggered pair of smaller mufflers. This example is missing its oval metal heat shields fitted on the head pipes at the point of contact with the rider's thigh. The seat on this mist green and white machine is the correct all-black form that the '67 Bonnie pictured previously should have had.

The 1968-70 model years are often called the most desirable for 650 Bonnevilles, and this gorgeous '68 shows why. The Hi-Fi Scarlet tank finish was split down its center by a silver stripe lined in gold, the fenders are polished stainless. A major upgrade on Triumph's 650s was the 8-in. twin-leading-shoe front brake, developed on the factory's production racers the previous year.

1968 electrical systems moved the Zener diode to underneath the headlamp, where it resided in the air stream behind a finned aluminum heat sink. The chromed ring on the left side of the front brake was for appearance only and fitted only to 1968 T120Rs and TR6s. The bike shown is missing its Minimum Oil Level oil-tank transfer and its scripted "Bonneville" tool box transfer.

This R-model Trophy was sold as a "touring" 650, hence its larger fuel tank. This was the last year for the tank-top parcel grids on U.S. models. Important details for restorers included the introduction of 12-point cylinder base nuts, revised primary covers with access covers to allow the engine to be timed with a strobe, and the Lucas ignition points now mounted on individually-adjustable plates.

During production of 1968 models the early machines came with ribbed Dunlop front tires and K70s on the rear. This arrangement was changed to K70s on both ends (3.25 x 19 front, 4.00 x 18 rear) part way through the production run. The new 7-in. Lucas headlamps featured relocated ammeter and idiot-lights, and their mounting brackets were now slotted for fore/aft adjustment.

'69 BONNIE

For 1969, Triumph sold Bonnevilles with three different fuel-tank paint designs, all using the orangish-red Olympic Flame with silver, outlined in white pinstriping. This example shows the second paint condition, with a single sweeping scallop rising from the top of the tank badge. This would be amended on the final version to include a second set of scallops curving down from the bottom of the badges.

The TLS front brake was given a bell-crank actuating arrangement, which improved its feel at the brake lever and also ended problems with the 1968 brake's straight-pull cable getting caught on the fender when the forks compressed. Girling rear shocks lost their spring shrouds for the '69 season. And Bonnies gained a real set of "windtone" horns, recognizable by their rounded covers.

'69 TR6R

More internal engine improvements came in 1969. A larger, heavier flywheel was added in an attempt to reduce vibration, and the camshafts were Nitrided at the factory for greater wear-resistance. Transmission gears also received a new hardening treatment. To attempt to finally put an end to leaky pushrod tubes, the tubes were sealed with Viton O-rings.

Triumph gave its twins exhaust balance pipes in 1969, the road models such as this Trophy Red TR6R having their cross pipe near the exhaust ports. This feature was proven to reduce noise while boosting performance. A new, cleaner-looking badge graced the fuel tanks. And the single-carb 650 roadsters were renamed Tigers, though long-time Triumph lovers still called them Trophies.

'70 BONNIE

With development of the 1971 oil-bearing frames, and new running gear nearing completion at BSA Group's R&D center, the 1970 Bonnies and TR6s were indeed the last of the "old school" classic Triumph twins. The T120R was a looker from any angle, and gained a new rear fender stay that included the rear passenger grab loop. More refinements to the gearbox proved troublesome in use.

Crankcase breather tube fixed to the left side of this 1970 Bonnie's rear fender was part of a new, more effective crankcase-scavenging system that vented the lower end into the primary chaincase. This arrangement was proven on the Trident and helped reduce oil leaks. This bike wears regular Lucas 6H horns sometimes fitted to Bonnies when supplies of the superior "windtone" units were delayed.

By 1970 Triumph's 650cc high-piper was no longer a competitive tool, but the Trophy carried on as a stylish street-scrambler. It wore the new exhaust system introduced in 1969, with a pair of roadster mufflers wrapped in a chrome-plated wire heat shield which Americans called the "barbeque grill." The Spring Gold paint had a black center stripe outlined in gold on the Trophy's 2-1/2-gallon tank.

Stainless steel fenders riding on black stays continued on the '70 Trophy 650, as did the standard center-mounted speedo. Buyers of the $1,300 machine could order it with either Dunlop K70 street tires or block-pattern Trials Universals. A wide-ratio gearbox was also available as a dealer-fitted option. Note the DOT-mandated orange side reflectors underneath the fuel tank, used since 1968.

Chapter Seven

Assemble & Restore the '63

The '63 is Reassembled into a Running Bike

Restoring and assembling the '63 Bonnie is a little different than the '69. According to Gary Chitwood, "The two frames are basically the same, except for the rear section. The '63 mounts the rear pegs on the mid-section of the frame, while on the '69 the pegs are mounted off engine plates. Of course the '63 uses a front fork with internal springs, while the '69 fork uses external springs. Another difference is the oil tank, on the '63 they used rubber washers, on the '69 it's actually rubber mounted. With the '63s, they had trouble with cracking on that upper mount."

There just aren't many motorcycles with the pure visual appeal of a really nice Bonneville or TR6 from the 1960s.

The parts for a 1963 Bonneville are compiled. This represents weeks of work with the chrome shop, paint shop and organizing the parts.

The front and rear fenders, gas tank, gas tank emblems, speedometer and tachometer for the '63 Bonneville.

The center stand springs are installed, shown is an old trick of the trade.

Here you can see the swingarm spacer.

The white paint used on the '63 is Alaskan white. Garry says he's old skool, "I still shoot lacquer, but in some parts of the country you can't buy it anymore. The paint, both the white and the gold stripe, comes from Don Hudson at Hudson Cycle.

"There are a few other changes. The headlight bucket for example. On the '63 it has just one hole for the ammeter, the '69 has four holes: one for the ammeter, one for the hi-low switch, and one each for the oil light and the high beam indicator. The '63 puts the ignition switch on the side cover and the '69 has it mounted in the headlight ear. And the exhaust is different because the pipes mount a little differently and the '69 uses a balance tube and the '63 does not. The 69 uses a

(continued on page 121)

The swing arm is installed to the frame. Like the other bike, a little paint may have to be filed away so the fork slides in easily.

The front and rear sections of the frame are shown here with the complete swing arm. We are now ready to assemble the shocks.

Garry and Bobby are putting in the rear frame section bolt.

The rear shock assembly is laid out and ready for installation.

A round file is used to clean out the area for the rear frame-section hardware bolt.

The top clips are placed on the rear shock, this is a two-person job as one person needs to compress the spring.

Here you can see Ryan and Garry hanging the right side shock absorber in place. The correct bolts for this year have "Bradleys" on the head.

Once the rear damper units are in place, Garry sets the lifting handle between the two shocks.

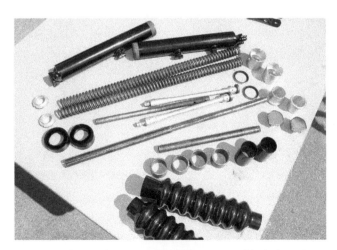

Here we have the parts needed to assembled the '63 front end, a lot more parts than on the '69.

Though shown on the '69, this tool can be used to pull the stanchion or fork tube up into the lug.

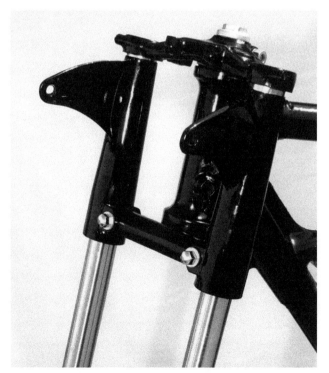

With the fork tubes in place the crew is ready to assemble the complete front end assembly. Note how the fork ears seem too short, this is correct.

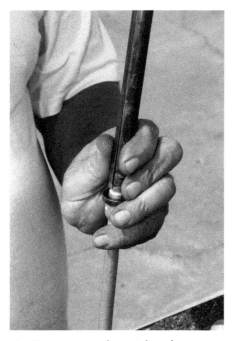

1. Garry snaps the guide tube onto the restrictor rod.

2. Close up shows how the guide tube and restrictor rod snap together.

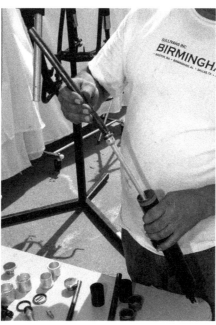

3. This is the end of the restrictor rod that goes into the lower leg, with the flanged bolt and washer screwed in place temporarily. The slot must line up correctly in the lower leg.

4. Here Garry drops the restrictor rod assembly down into the lower fork leg (or bottom member).

5. Now the flanged bolt, with sealing washer, is tightened to the restrictor, be sure the slot (seen in photo number 3) for the drain plug is lined up. Remember the black silicone, as mentioned in the other ass'm.

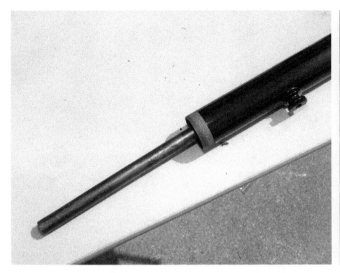

Here we have the lower member with the restrictor rod assembly installed.

Garry holds the cap nut with the guide pin inserted part way.

The pin is used to hold the upper guide tube into the cap nut.

Always use a seal drive to install the fork seal into the dust excluder.

Next, tap the upper cap into the dust excluder, use a little light oil to ease the installation.

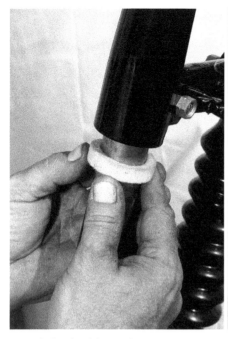

We slide the felt washer up into the stanction cover. These can also be made from rubber.

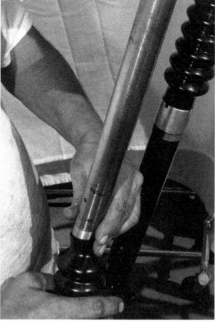

Next, spray the stanchion with light oil and slide the telescopic gaiter up into place.

After installing the gaiter Garry puts the dust excluder sleeve nut assembly on.

Rub more light oil on the stanchion before sliding the lower member on.

With the bushing and damping sleeve in place it's time to slide the lower member up to the dust excluder.

Be sure to use the special tool to install the dust excluder, don't use a pipe wrench or hammer and chisel.

shorter muffler too. For carburetors, the '63 uses monoblocs, while the '69 comes with the Amal concentrics. And one of the most obvious differences is in the gas tanks, the '63 has the four-gallon tank and by '69 the Bonneville came with the slim-line three gallon tank. Another obvious difference, but one you can't see, is the electrical system. The '63 is a 6-volt bike and by '69 the Triumphs were all 12 volts (Triumph converted all the bikes to 12 volts in '66)."

"Another fairly obvious difference is the front brake, the '63 uses one leading and one trailing shoe. In '68 Triumph started using the twin leading-shoe brake, and you can see the difference because of the linkage on the backing plate. One more change that's less obvious is the fenders. On the '63 the front fender is a painted alloy fender while the rear is steel. On the '69 Bonnie both of the fenders are steel. So even though the bikes look very similar, there are a number of differences in the two machines."

GAUGES

People often think that Triumphs used the same, or nearly the same, gauges throughout the 60s, but in reality the gauges changed quite a bit over the years, though the overall look remained similar. The '63 for example is the last one to use Smith's chronometric gauges. In '63 the speedometer read all the way to 140 miles per hour while the TR6 only promised the rider 120. When it comes to repairing a pair of old gauges, Garry Chitwood has a few tips to pass along (surprise). "With the chronometric gauges I usually fix them myself, because you can get the bezel off. The later gauges, like those on the '69, require a special de-crimp tool to do a nice job of disassembly. Those gauges I send out, usually to Nisonger in New York, they do a nice job. If the face is faded or the paint is flaking, you can buy just a face for many of the gauges, Mitch Klempf has them and I think John Healy at Coventry Spares has them too. Some of the gauges used different ratios, so that even if you don't care about a perfect restoration, you still can't just grab a gauge for one year and use it on another."

1. Now it's time to install the instrument bracket to the top lug, the bolts should have a smooth head. Later Triumphs have a small circle in the center of the bolt.

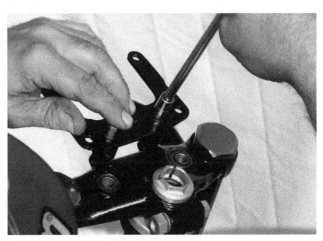

2. Fully tighten the bracket...

3. ...before installing the speedometer.

The 1963 speedometer and tachometer are mounted to the top lug.

Here we have the pieces that make up the steering damper assembly. Don't forget the aluminum washer, seen under the knob in Bobby's right hand.

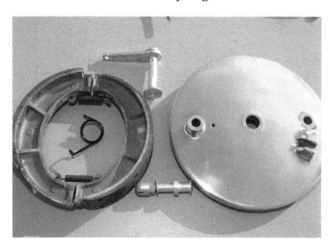

The anchor plate and brake assembly.

The spring plate, friction plate and anchor plate are installed. A locating pin will be inserted later into the notch seen next to his thumb.

The steering damper rod is installed and ready for adjustment.

The lever return spring and the brake cam lever are assembled. We powder-coat the spring for durability.

The dust cover is taped down before the circlip is installed in the front wheel.

The brake shoes are placed together with the anchor plate.

The anchor plates with the brakes are now installed to the drum.

The front wheel bearing is installed.

The front wheel is ready for placement.

The rear tire goes on to the tire rim a little help from Armor-All.

Bobby reaches inside the tire to set the rim locks in place.

Rim locks are in place and the tire is half on, we're ready for the inner tube.

Placing the tube inside the tire, insert the valve stem first to hold the tire in place.

Rim lock nut and washer.

The inner tube gets placed in the rear wheel.

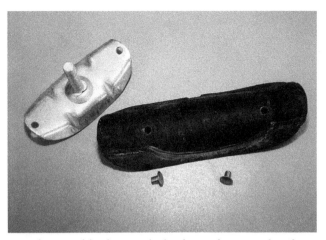

We disassemble the rim locks, have them re-plated...

Using a tire spoon, Bobby finishes mounting the tire on the rim, plenty of Armor-All helps the tire slide over the rim.

...and then put them back together again...

Take it slow, you don't want to chip the chrome. Sometimes we wrap the tire tool in tape, and it helps to let the tire warm in the sun before installation.

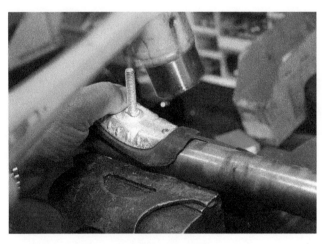

...with fresh rivets from the hardware store.

The rim lock nut is tightened.

Here's the complete front end of our 1963.

The fender bridge is bolted to lower the fork leg.

The rear fender, number plate, and brake light assembly.

Detail shot shows the fender mount.

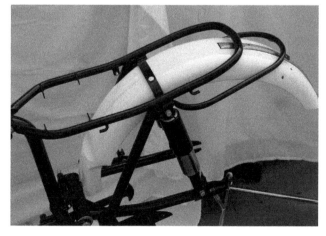

The complete rear fender to the rear section.

The brake light assembly and the number plate are joined.

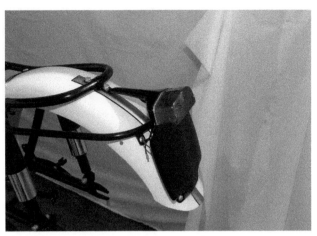

The brake light assembly is mounted to the rear fender.

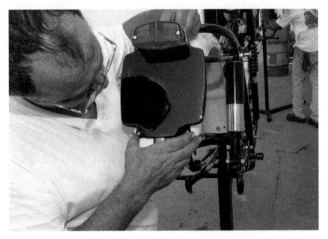

Installing the number plate and brake light assembly to the rear fender.

Tail light wires are routed as shown.

Using 1/4 inch bolts, the rear grab rail is installed on the rear fender.

The rear hub and hardware.

The rear wheel assembly and all of its parts.

The brake hub, brake shoes, and parts.

The distance piece is installed to the rear axle.

LACING AND TRUING WHEELS

Truing wheels is one of those acquired skills. In a perfect world the wheel is completely disassembled, the spokes go out for new cad plating, the nipples are replaced with new chrome units, and the rim is likewise sent out for new plating. Stainless spokes are available and while not totally accurate, some people really like the extra sparkle.

Reassembly requires patience and experience. "You have to have a truing stand and a dial indicator," explains Garry Chitwood. "All these wheels use 40-spokes. If you haven't done it before, set an already laced wheel near the one you're trying to reassemble and you can just copy the pattern. I do the initial adjusting with a screw driver, turning the nipples from the slot on the back of each one. Sometimes the spokes are too long, and you have to grind off any excess that sticks out past the edge of the nipple or it will poke a hole in the tube. Once I have the rim close I adjust both the side-to-side runout, and the radial runout, to no more than .005 inch. The rear rims have to be laced with some offset to clear the chain, the manuals list the amount of offset for each year. You might want to take the rim to an experienced shop for the final adjusting if you haven't done this before, it can be very frustrating."

The brake plate is installed to the rear wheel hub.

The axle is spaced out.

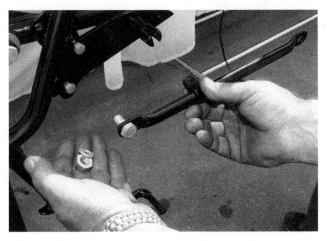

The brake torque stay is ready to be installed.

The wheel is mounted as well as the chain guard.

The chain guard and hardware.

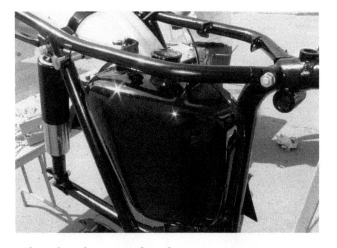

The oil tank mounted to the rear section.

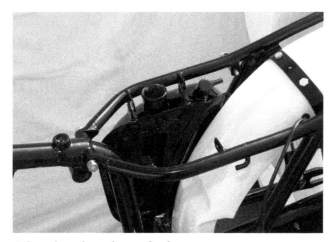

The oil tank and rear fender.

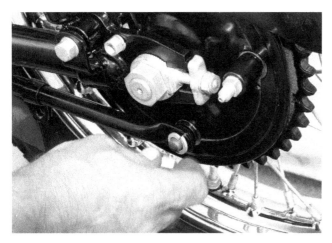

The rear torque stay is mounted to the brake plate.

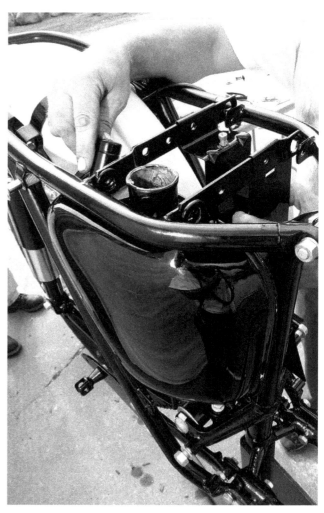

The battery straps and the battery box are installed.

The complete rolling chassis.

These are the spigot rubbers and the correct stepped bolts used to mount the front and rear strap.

Lighting and ignition switch.

Here is one of the rubbers being slipped into place.

The side cover is placed.

The long strap for the battery box is mounted.

The horn and mounting brackets.

Complete battery box assembly.

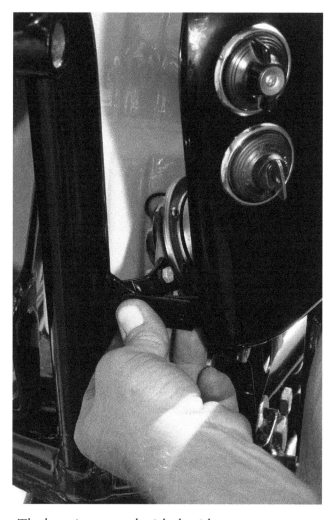

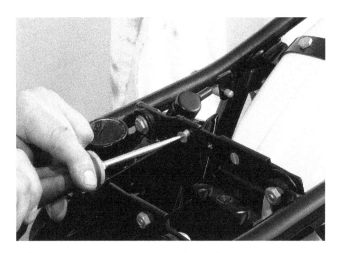

The screws are installed for the tool bag.

The horn is mounted with the side cover.

The installed battery box and tool tray.

The front motor bolt is installed.

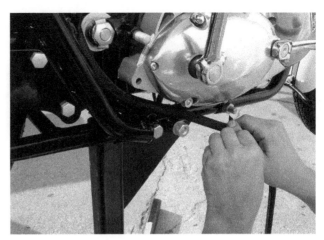

The oil lines are cut to length to the oil tank and the motor.

The motor, frame and wheels all come together.

The oil tank filter line is installed to the motor and routed as shown.

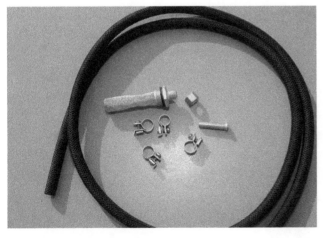

The oil line, oil filter, and clips.

The right side rear engine plate is mounted.

The left side exhaust pipe is installed, the '63 does not use a connector pipe.

Taking precautions to correctly route the exhaust pipe, they don't just fall into the right position.

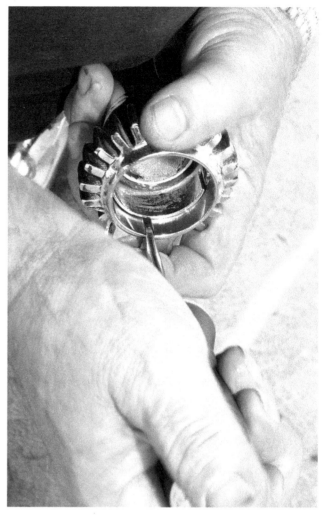

Here we are spreading open the clamp to help it slide over the header pipe.

The rear wheel completed.

The complete 1963.

The complete rocker boxes ready to go on the bike.

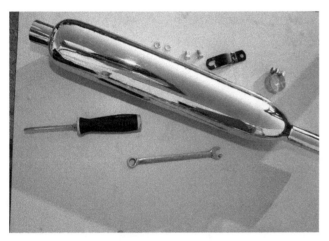
Muffler, bracket, and hardware.

The front rocker box is installed.

The muffler bracket and clip are mounted to the muffler.

Our two Amal monobloc carburetors.

The right side carburetor is installed.

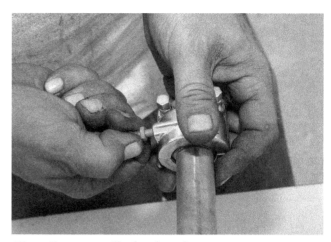

Here Garry installs the throttle stop.

6-volt coils mounted to the frame as shown.

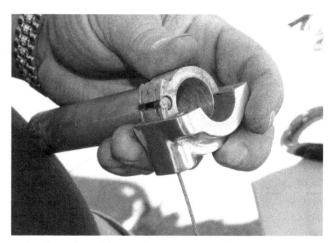

The throttle cables and throttle assembly are installed in a number of steps.

The twist grip assembly, the housing is aluminum and was polished to bring out the shine.

Garry slides the throttle assembly into place, grease up the handlebar so it's sure to rotate freely.

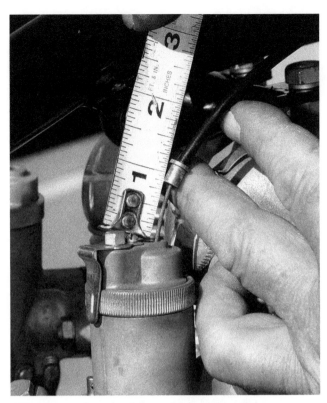

The correct length of the cable is measured.

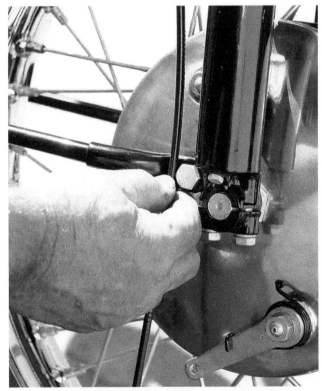

The length of the front brake cable is checked for accuracy.

The right lever and brake cable are installed to the handle bars.

Throttle cable assembly.

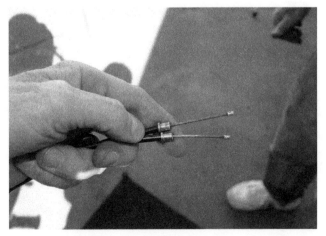

Shown here is the correct length for the throttle cables.

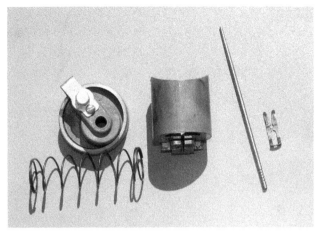

The throttle valve, needle jet, needle clip, spring, and mixing chamber cap.

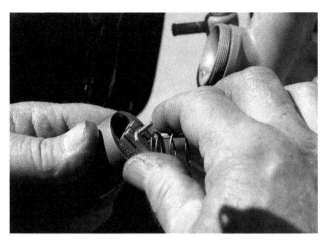

The throttle cable is installed with the throttle valve.

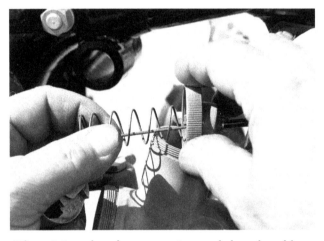

The mixing chamber cap spring and throttle cable.

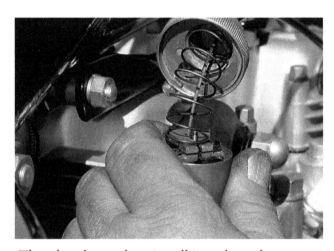

Throttle valve ready to install into the carburetor.

The throttle cable end is slipped into the throttle valve.

The carburetor and throttle cables completely assembled.

The headlight bucket ready for wiring.

The headlight wires are connected to the main harness.

With the wiring completed, the headlight is reseated.

Color code wires for the contact breaker points.

This rectifier came off the original bike, we decided to re-install it as it's genuine Lucas and still works.

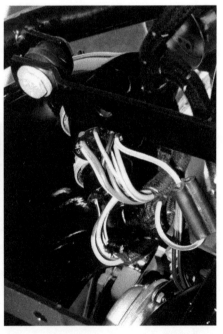

The wiring for the ignition switch and lighting.

139

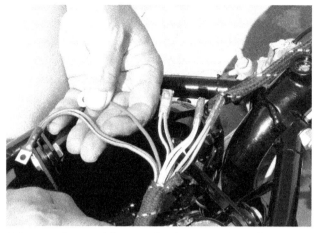

The rectifier and battery leads are ready to be hooked up.

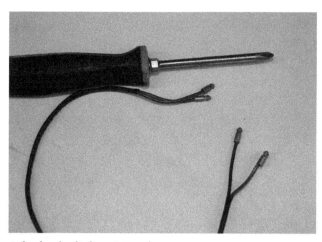

The brake light wiring harness.

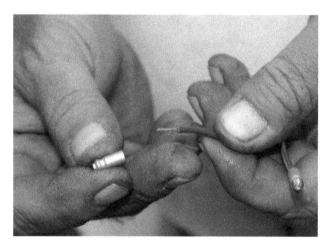

A bullet connector is placed at the of the wire.

Completed rectifier and wires.

The connectors are soldered.

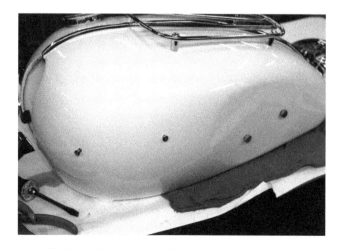

Install the styling strip and then the parcel grid. Check all the fasteners to make sure they thread into the tank properly.

With the gas tank newly painted, emblems are carefully placed.

You might have to clean any overspray from the hole before installing the new fork lock.

The old rivet may need to be drilled out before a new one can be installed.

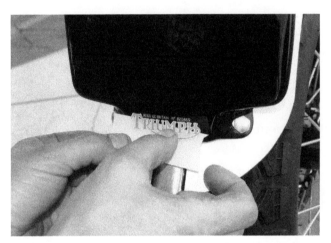

A final touch, the Triumph transfer decal is added to the number plate.

We just use regular hardware-store pop-rivets to install the fork-lock cover.

The completed 1963 Bonneville.

Books from Wolfgang Publications can be found at select book stores and numerous web sites.

Titles	ISBN	Price	# of pages
Advanced Airbrush Art	9781929133208	$27.95	144 pages
Advanced Custom Motorcycle Assembly & Fabrication	9781929133239	$27.95	144 pages
Advanced Custom Motorcycle Wiring - *Revised*	9781935828761	$27.95	144 pages
Advanced Pinstripe Art	9781929133321	$27.95	144 pages
Advanced Sheet Metal Fab	9781929133123	$27.95	144 pages
Advanced Tattoo Art - *Revised*	9781929133822	$27.95	144 pages
Airbrush How-To with Mickey Harris	9781929133505	$27.95	144 pages
Barris: Flames, Scallops and Striping	9781929133550	$24.95	144 pages
Bean're - Motorcycle Nomad	9781935828709	$18.95	256 pages
Body Painting	9781929133666	$27.95	144 pages
Building Hot Rods	9781929133437	$27.95	144 pages
Colorful World of Tattoo Models	9781935828716	$34.95	144 pages
Composite Materials 1	9781929133765	$27.95	144 pages
Composite Materials 2	9781929133932	$27.95	144 pages
Composite Materials 3	9781935828662	$27.95	144 pages
Composite Materials Step by Step Projects	9781929133369	$27.95	144 pages
Cultura Tattoo Sketchbook	9781935828839	$32.95	284 pages
Custom Bike Building Basics	9781935828624	$24.95	144 pages
Custom Motorcycle Fabrication	9781935828792	$27.95	144 pages
George the Painter	9781935828815	$18.95	256 pages
Harley-Davidson Sportster Hop-Up & Customizing Guide	9781935828952	$27.95	144 pages
Harley-Davidson Sportser Buell Engine Hop-Up Guide	9781929133093	$24.95	144 pages
How Airbrushes Work	9781929133710	$24.95	144 pages
Honda Enthusiast Guide Motorcycles 1959-1985	9781935828853	$27.95	144 pages
How-To Airbrush, Pinstripe & Goldleaf	9781935828693	$27.95	144 pages
How-To Airbrush Pin-ups	9781929133802	$27.95	144 pages
How-To Build Old Skool Bobber - 2nd Edition	9781935828785	$27.95	144 pages

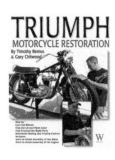

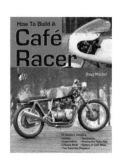

Books from Wolfgang Publications can be found at select book stores and numerous web sites.

Titles	ISBN	Price	# of pages
How-To Build a Cheap Chopper	9781929133178	$27.95	144 pages
How-To Build Cafe Racer	9781935828730	$27.95	144 pages
How-To Chop Tops	9781929133499	$24.95	144 pages
How-To Draw Monsters	9781935828914	$27.95	144 pages
How-To Fix American V-Twin	9781929133727	$27.95	144 pages
How-To Paint Tractors & Trucks	9781929133475	$27.95	144 pages
Hot Rod Wiring	9781929133987	$27.95	144 pages
Into the Skin	9781935828174	$34.95	144 pages
Kosmoski's *New* Kustom Paint Secrets	9781929133833	$27.95	144 pages
Learning the English Wheel	9781935828891	$27.95	144 pages
Mini Ebooks - Butterfly and Roses	9781935828167	Ebook Only	
Mini Ebooks - Skulls & Hearts	9781935828198	Ebook Only	
Mini Ebooks - Lettering & Banners	9781935828204	Ebook Only	
Mini Ebooks - Tribal Stars	9781935828211	Ebook Only	
Pin-Ups on Two Wheels	9781929133956	$29.95	144 pages
Pro Pinstripe	9781929133925	$27.95	144 pages
Sheet Metal Bible	9781929133901	$29.95	176 pages
Sheet Metal Fab Basics B&W	9781929133468	$24.95	144 pages
Sheet Metal Fab for Car Builders	9781929133383	$27.95	144 pages
SO-CAL Speed Shop, Hot Rod Chassis	9781935828860	$27.95	144 pages
Tattoo Bible #1	9781929133840	$27.95	144 pages
Tattoo Bible #2	9781929133857	$27.95	144 pages
Tattoo Bible #3	9781935828754	$27.95	144 pages
Tattoo Lettering Bible	9781935828921	$27.95	144 pages
Tattoo Sketchbook / Nate Power	9781935828884	$27.95	144 pages
Tattoo Sketchbook, Jim Watson	9781935828037	$32.95	112 pages
Triumph Restoration - Pre Unit	9781929133635	$29.95	144 pages
Triumph Restoration - Unit 650cc	9781929133420	$29.95	144 pages
Vintage Dirt Bikes - Enthusiast's Guide	9781929133314	$27.95	144 pages
Ult Sheet Metal Fab	9780964135895	$24.95	144 pages
Ultimate Triumph Collection	9781935828655	$49.95	144 pages

 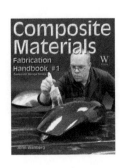  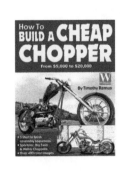 

Sources

Baxter Cycle
400 Lincoln
Marne, IA
712 781 2351
www.baxtercycle.com

Chitwood, Garry
can be contacted by mail at:
Sullivans Birmingham
5921 Greenwood parkway
Bessemer, AL 35023
1 276 734 5736

Coventry Spares Ltd.
John Healy
15 Abbey Lane,
Middleboro, MA 02346
1 800 451 5113

Hudson Cycle
Wakefield, MA
Don Hudson

Mitch Klempf
Klempf's British Parts
61589 210 Ave
Dodge Center, MN 55927
507 374 2222
www.klempfs.com

Sullivan, Bobby
can be contacted by mail at:
Sullivans
121 Franklin
Hanson, MA 02341

Shadley Brothers/Auto-Tec
1125 Bedford, Route 18
Whitman, MA 02382
781 447 2403

Credits
Bike owners, at time photos were taken,
by page number.
90 Boyd Uzzell
91 Dick Brown
92 Mike Whitney, photo Jeff Hackett
93 Dave Flory
94 Baxter Cycle
95 Bobby Sullivan
96 Bobby Sullivan
97 Jim Hess
98 Bobby Sullivan
99 Bobby Sullivan
100 Baxter Cycle
101 Mark Jensen
102 Baxter Cycle
103 Bobby Sullivan
104 Denny Narland
105 Bobby Sullivan
106 Bobby Sullivan
107 Baxter Cycle
108 Bobby Sullivan
109 Bobby Sullivan
110 Bobby Sullivan
111 Denny Narland
112 Baxter Cycle
113 Baxter Cycle

CPSIA information can be obtained
at www.ICGtesting.com
Printed in the USA
BVHW020211170619
551180BV00010B/40/P